James M. Macoun

Check List of Canadian Plants

James M. Macoun

Check List of Canadian Plants

ISBN/EAN: 9783337187040

Printed in Europe, USA, Canada, Australia, Japan

Cover: Foto ©Andreas Hilbeck / pixelio.de

More available books at **www.hansebooks.com**

CHECK LIST

OF

CANADIAN PLANTS.

BY

JAMES M. MACOUN,

Assistant Botanist to the Geological and Natural History Survey of Canada.

OTTAWA:

PRINTED BY CUNNINGHAM & LINDSAY.

1889.

ERRATA.

Page 7.—For "Nuphar pygmæa, Salisb." read "Nymphæa pygmæa, Salisb."
" 7.—For "Saraceniaceæ and Saracenia" read "Sarraceniaceæ and Sarracenia."
" 7.—For "Papaver Rheas" read "Papaver Rhæas."
" 16.—For "Gleditschi" read "Gleditschia."
" 18.—For "Sarothammus" read "Sarothamnus."
" 19.—After "Cratægus coccinea, L." insert "var. macrantha."
" 19.—For "Pirus Acuparia" read "Pirus Aucuparia."
" 20.—For "Rosa acicularis, var. Bourgeaniana," read "Bourgeauiana."
" 22.—For "Saxifraga azoides" read "Saxifraga aizoides."
" 23.—For "Epilobium minutum, var. folisum," read "var. foliosum."
" 24.—For "Anthruscus" read "Anthriscus."
" 25.—For "Peucednaum" read "Peucedanum."

NOTE.

The basis of this Check-list has been Professor John Macoun's Catalogue of Canadian Plants. Where a name is printed in brackets it signifies, not that it is a synonym of the one immediately above it, although this is generally the case, but that, where specimens have been so named in Professor Macoun's Catalogue, they are now known by the name given in the list.

LIST OF CANADIAN PLANTS.

RANUNCULACEÆ.

ACONITUM

Columbianum, Nutt.
(A. Fischeri, Reich.)
Napellus, L., var. delphinifolium,
Seringe.

ACTÆA

alba, Bigel.
spicata, L., var. arguta, Torr.
var. rubra, Ait.

ANEMONE

acutiloba, Lawson.
cylindrica, Gray.
deltoidea, Hook.
dichotoma, L.
Drummondii, Watson.
Hepatica, L.
multifida, Poir.
narcissiflora, L.
nemorosa, L.
nudicaulis, Gray.
parviflora, Michx.
patens, L., var. Nuttalliana, Gray
occidentalis, Watson.
Richardsoni, Hook.
Virginiana, L.

ANEMONELLA

thalictroides, Spach.
(Thalictrum anemonoides,
Michx.)

AQUILEGIA

brevistyla, Hook.
Canadensis, L.
flavescens, Watson.
formosa, Fisch.
vulgaris, L.

CALTHA

biflora, DC.
(C. palustris, L., var. minima,
Regel.)
leptosepala, DC.
natans, Pall.
palustris, L.
var. Sibirica, Regel.

CIMICIFUGA

elata, Nutt.
racemosa, Nutt.

CLEMATIS

Douglasii, Hook.
ligusticifolia, Nutt.
var. brevifolia, Nutt.
verticillaris, DC.
var. Columbiana, Gray.
Virginiania, L.

TRUTVETTERIA
grandis, Nutt.

TROLLIUS
laxus, Salisb.

MAGNOLIACEÆ.

LIRIODENDRON
Tulipifera, L.

MAGNOLIA
acuminata, L.

ANONACEÆ.

ASIMINA
triloba, Dunal.

MENISPERMACEÆ.

MENISPERMUM
Canadense, L.

BERBERIDACEÆ.

ACHLYS
triphylla, DC.

BERBERIS
Aquifolium, Pursh.
nervosa, Pursh.
repens, Lindl.
vulgaris, L.

CAULOPHYLLUM
thalictroides, Michx.

JEFFERSONIA
diphylla, Pers.

PODOPHYLLUM
peltatum, L.

VANCOUVERIA
hexandra, Morr. & Decne.

NYMPHÆACEÆ.

BRASENIA
peltata, Pursh.

NELUMBIUM
luteum, Willd.

NUPHAR
advena, Ait.
Kalmianum, Ait.
(N. pumilum, Smith.)
polysepalum, Engelm.
pygmæa, Salisb.
rubrodiscum, Morong,
(N. luteum, Smith.)

NYMPHÆA
odorata, Ait.
var. minor, Sims.
tuberosa, Paine.

SARACENIACEÆ.

SARACENIA
purpurea, L.
var. heterophylla, Torr.

PAPAVERACEÆ.

CHELIDONIUM
majus, L.

PAPAVER
nudicaule, L.
Rheas, L.
somniferum, L.,

PLATYSTIGMA
Oreganum, Benth. & Hook.

SANGUINARIA
Canadensis, L.

FUMARIACEÆ.

ADLUMIA
cirrhosa, Raf.

CORYDALIS
aurea, Willd.
    var. occidentalis, Gray.
flavula, DC.

DICENTRA
Canadensis, DC.
Cucullaria, DC.
formosa, DC.

FUMARIA
officinalis, L.
parviflora, L.

CRUCIFERÆ.

ALYSSUM
calycinum, L.

ARABIS
alpina, L.
Canadensis, L.

canescens, Nutt., var. latifolia,
    Watson,
confinis Wat.
    (A. Drummondii, Gray, var.)
      brachycarpa, Gray.
Drummondii, Gray.
hirsuta, Scop.
Holbœllii, Hornem.

humifusa, Wat., var. pubescens
    Wat.
    (A. petræa, Lam.)
lævigata, Poir.　.
Lyallii, Watson.
lyrata, L.
    var. occidentalis, Wat.
    (A. petræa, Lam. var. ambigua,
      Regel,)
perfoliata, Lam.
stricta, Huds.

BARBAREA
vulgaris, R. Br.
    var. arcuata, Koch.
    var. stricta, Regel.
glauca, Pursh.
pauciflora, Pursh.
Scouleri, Hook.

BRASSICA
alba, Gray.
campestris, L.
nigra, Koch,
Rapa, L.
Sinapistrum, Boiss.

BRAYA
alpina. Sternb., var. Ameri-
    cana, Hook.
    var. glabella, Watson.
Eschscholtziana, B. & H.
pilosa, Hook.

CAKILE
Americana, Nutt.

CAMELINA
sativa, Crantz.

CAPSELLA
Bursa-pastoris, Mœnch.
divaricata, Walp.

CARDAMINE
angulata, Hook.
bellidifolia, L.
hirsuta, L.
  var. sylvatica, Gray.
oligosperma, Nutt.
pratensis, L.
  var. occidentalis, Wat.
purpurea, Cham. & Schl.
rhomboidea, DC.
  var. purpurea, Torr.
rotundifolia, Michx.

CHEIRANTHUS
asper, Cham. & Schlecht.
pygmæus, Adams.

COCHLEARIA
Anglica, L.
Danica, L.
officinalis, L.
tridactylites, Banks.

DENTARIA
diphylla, Michx.
heterophylla, Nutt.
laciniata, Muhl.
maxima, Nutt.
tenella, Pursh.

DIPLOTAXIS
muralis DC.
tenuifolia, DC.

DRABA
alpina, L.
  var. algida, Regel.
  var. (?) corymbosa, Durand.
  var. glacialis, Dickie.
  var. hebecarpa, Lindb.
  var. (?) mircropetala, Durand,
androsacea, Wahl.
arabisans, Michx.
aurea, Vahl.

Caroliniana, Walt.
crassifolia, Grah.
hirta, L.
hyperborea, Desv.
  var. siliquosa, Gray.
incana, L.
  var. borealis, T. & G.
  var. confusa, Poir.
nemorosa, L, var. hebecarpa,
      Lindb.
  var. leiocarpa, Lindb.
rupestris, R. Br.
stellata, Jacq.
  var. hebecarpa, DC.
  var. Johannis, Regel.
  var. nivalis, Regel.
stenoloba, Ledeb.
verna, L.

EUTREMA
Edwardsii, R. Br.

ERYSIMUM
asperum, DC.
cheiranthoides, L.
parviflorum, Nutt.
orientale, R. Br.

HESPERIS
matronalis, L.

LEPIDIUM
campestre, R. Br.
Draba, L.
intermedium, Gray.
Menziesii, DC.
ruderale, L.
sativum, L.
Virginicum, L.

NASTURTIUM
amphibium, R. Br
Armoracia, Fries.
curvisiliqua, Nutt.

lacustre, Gray.
obtusum, Nutt.
officinale, R. Br.
palustre, DC.
  var, hispidum, F. & M.
trachycarpum, Gray.

NESLIA
paniculata, Desv.

PARRYA
arctica, R. Br.
arenicola, Hook. f.
nudicaulis, var. aspera, Regel.
  var. glabra, Regel.

PHYSARIA
didymocarpa, Gray.

PLATYSPERMUM
scapigerum, Hook.

RAPHANUS
Raphanistrum, L.
sativus, L.

SENEBIERA
Coronopus, Poir.
didyma, Pers.

SISYMBRIUM
acutangulum, DC.
canescens, Nutt.
  var. brachycarpum, Wats.
humile, C. A. Meyer.
incisum. Engelm.
  var. filipes, Gray.
  var, Hartwegianum, Wats.
linifolium, Nutt.
officinale, Scop.
salsugineum, Pall.
Sophia, L.
  var. (S. sophioides, Fisch.)
Thaliana, Gay.

SMELOWSKIA
calycina, C. A. Meyer.

SUBULARIA
aquatica, L.

THELYPODIUM
pinnatifidum, Watson.

THLASPI
alpestre, L.
arvense, L.

THYSANOCARPUS
curvipes, Hook.
pusillus, Hook.

VESICARIA
alpina, Nutt.
arctica, Richards.
Ludoviciana, DC.

CAPPARIDACEÆ.

CLEOME
integrifolia, T. & G.
lutea, Hook.

POLANISIA
graveolens, Raf.
uniglandulosa, DC.

CISTACEÆ.

HELIANTHEMUM
Canadense, Michx.

HUDSONIA
ericoides, L.
tomentosa, Nutt.

LECHEA

major, Michx.
minor, Walt.
thymifolia, Pursh.

VIOLACEÆ.

SOLEA

concolor, Ging.
(Ionidium concolor, Benth. &
Hook.

VIOLA

biflora, L.
blanda, Willd.
var. renifolia, Gray.
(V. renifolia. Gray.)
Canadensis, L.
canina, L., var. adunca, Gray.
(var. longipes, Gray.)
(var. rupestris, Regel.)
var. Muhlenbergii, Gray.
(var. sylvestris, Regel.)
glabella, Nutt.
lanceolata, L.
Langsdorffii, Fisch.
Nuttallii, Pursh.
(var. linguæfolia, Nutt.)
odorata, L.
palmata, L.
(V. cucullata, Ait, var. palmata,
Gray.)
var. cucullata, Gray.
(V. cucullata, Ait.)
(V. cucullata, Ait, var. cordata,
Gray.)
palustris, L.
pedata, L.
pedatifida, Don.
(V. delphinifolia, Nutt.)
præmorsa, Dougl.
(V. Nuttallii, Pursh, var. præmorsa Wat.)
primulifolia, L.
pubescens, Ait.

(var. eriocarpa, Nutt.)
var. scabriuscula, T. & G.
rostrata, Muhl.
rotundifolia, Michx.
sagittata, Ait.
sarmentosa, Dougl.
Selkirkii, Pursh.
striata, Ait.
tricolor, L. var. arvensis, DC.

POLYGALACEÆ.

POLYGALA

incarnata, L.
paucifolia, Willd.
polygama, Walt.
sanguinea, L.
Senega, L.
verticillata, L.

CARYOPHYLLACEÆ.

ARENARIA

arctica, Stev.
var. breviscapa, Regel.
biflora, Watson, var. obtusa, Wat.
capillaris, Poir,, var. nardifolia,
Regel.
congesta, Nutt., var. subcongesta,
Watson.
Grœnlandica, Spreng.
lateriflora, L.
macrocarpa, Pursh.
macrophylla, Hook.
Michauxii, Hook. f.
peploides, L.
var. oblongifolia. Watson.
physodes, DC.
pungens, Nutt.
serpyllifolia, L.
stricta, Watson.
tenella, Nutt.
verna, L.
var. hirta, Watson.
var. rubella, Hook. f.

CERASTIUM
alpinum, L.
  var. Behringianum, Regel.
  var. Fischerianum, T. & G.

  var. glabratum, Hook.
  var. latifolium, Smith. (?)
arvense, L.
nutans, Raf.
oblongifolium, Torr.
pilosum, Ledeb.
trigynum, Vill.
viscosum, L.
vulgatum, L.

DIANTHUS
alpinus, L., var. repens, Regel.
Armeria, L.

LEPIGONUM (*Spergularia.*)
macrothecum, Fisch & Mey.
medium, Fries.
  var. macrocarpum, Watson.
rubrum, Fries.
  var. campestris, Gray.
salinum, Fries.

LYCHNIS
affinis, Vahl.
alpina, L.
apetala, L.
  var. glabra, Regel.
dioica, L.
Drummondii, Watson.
elata, Watson. (?)
Githago, Lam.
Flos-cuculi, L.
montana, Watson.
vespertina, Sibth.

SAGINA
decumbens, T. & G.
Linnæi, Presl.
nodosa, E. Meyer.

occidentalis, Watson.
procumbens, L.

SAPONARIA
officinalis, L.
Vaccaria, L.

SILENE
acaulis, L.
antirrhina, L.
Armeria, L.
Douglasii, Hook.
Gallica, L.
inflata, Sm.
Menziesii, Hook.
multicaulis, Nutt.
noctiflora, L.
nocturna, L.
Pennsylvanica, Michx. (?)
Scouleri, Hook.
stellata, Ait. f.
Virginica, L.

SPERGULA
arvensis, L.

STELLARIA
borealis, Bigel.
  var. alpestris, Gray.
calycantha, Bongard. (?)
crassifolia, Ehrh.
crispa, Cham. & Schlecht.
graminea, L.
gracilis, Richards.
humifusa, Rottb.
longifolia, Muhl.
longipes, Goldie.
  var. Edwardsii, T & G.
  var. læta, T. & G.
  var. minor, Hook.
media, Sm.
nitens, Nutt.
obtusa, Eng.
uliginosa, Murr.
umbellata, Turcz.

PARONYCHIEÆ.

ANYCHIA
dichotoma, Michx.

PARONYCHIA
sessiliflora, Nutt.

SCLERANTHUS
annuus, L.

PORTULACACEÆ.

CALANDRINIA
Menziesii, Hook.
pygmæa, Gray.
Vancouverensis, Macoun,

CLAYTONIA
Caroliniana, Michx.
  var. sessilifolia, Torr.
Chamissonis, Esch.
dichotoma, Nutt.
exigua, T. & G.
linearis, Dougl.
megarrhiza, Parry.
parvifolia, Moc.
perfoliata, Donn.
  var. parviflora, Torr.
  var. spathulata, Watson.
sarmentosa, C. A. Meyer.
Sibirica, L.
Virginica, L.

LEWISIA
rediviva, Pursh.

MONTIA
fontana, L.

PORTULACA
oleracea, L.

SPRAGUEA
umbellata, Torr.

TALINUM
spinescens, Torr.

ELATINEÆ.

ELATINE
Americana, Arnott.

HYPERICACEÆ.

ELODEA
campanulata, Pursh.
(E. Virginica, Nutt.)

HYPERICUM
anagalloides, Cham. & Schl.
Ascyron, L.
(H. pyramidatum, Ait.)
Canadense, L.
  var. major, Gray.
ellipticum, Hook.
formosum, HBK., var. Scouleri,
  Coulter.
(H. Scouleri, Hook.)
Kalmianum, L.
maculatum, Walt.
(H. corymbosum, Muhl.)
mutilum, L.
nudicaule, Walt.
(H. Sarotha, Michx.
perforatum, L.

MALVACEÆ.

ABUTILON
Avicennæ, Gærtn.

HIBISCUS
Moscheutos, L.
Trionum, L.

MALVA

borealis, Wallm.
crispa, L.
moschata, L.
rotundifolia, L.
sylvestris, L.

MALVASTRUM

coccineum, Gray.
Munroanum, Gray.

SIDA

hederacea, Torr. (?)

SIDALCEA

malvæflora, Gray.
Oregana, Gray,

SPHÆRALCEA

acerifolia, Nutt.
(S. rivularis, Torr.)

TILIACEÆ.

TILIA

Americana, L.
    var. pubescens, Loud
Europœa, L.

LINACEÆ.

LINUM

Catharticum, L.
perenne, L.
rigidum, Pursh.
striatum, Walt.
sulcatum, Riddell.
usitatissimum, L.
Virginianum, L.

GERANIACEÆ.

ERODIUM

cicutarium, L'Her.
moschatum, Willd.

FLŒRKEA

proserpinacoides, Willd.

GERANIUM

Carolinianum, L.
dissectum, L.
erianthum, DC.
incisum, Nutt.
(G. Fremonti, Torrey.)
maculatum, L.
molle, L.
pratense, L.
pusillum, L.
Richardsoni, Fisch. & Mey.
Robertianum, L.

IMPATIENS

fulva, Nutt.
pallida, Nutt.

LIMNANTHES

Douglasii, R. Br.

OXALIS

Acetosella, L.
corniculata, L.
    var. stricta, Sav.
Oregana, Nutt.

RUTACEÆ.

PTELEA

trifoliata, L.

XANTHOXYLUM

Americanum, Mill.

ILICINEÆ.

ILEX

glabra, Gray.
opaca, Ait. (?)
verticillata, Gray.

NEMOPANTHES

Canadensis, DC.

CELASTRACEÆ.

CELASTRUS

scandens, L.

EUONYMUS

Americanus, L., var. obovatus,
T. & G.
atropurpureus, Jacq.

PACHYSTIMA

Myrsinites, Raf.

RHAMNACEÆ.

CEANOTHUS

Americanus, L.
ovatus, Desf.
sanguineus, Pursh.
velutinus, Dougl.
var. lævigatus, T. & G.

RHAMNUS

alnifolia, L'Her.
Cathartica, L.
Purshiana, DC

VITACEÆ.

AMPELOPSIS

quinquefolia, Michx.

VITIS

æstivalis, Michx.
(V. Labrusca, L.)
cordifolia, Lam.
riparia, Michx.

SAPINDACEÆ.

ACER

circinatum, Pursh,
dasycarpum, Ehrh.
glabrum, Torr.
macrophyllum, Pursh.
Pennsylvanicum, L.
rubrum, L.
saccharinum, Wangenh.
var. nigrum, T. & G.
spicatum, Lam.

ÆSCULUS

Hippocastanum, L.

NEGUNDO

aceroides, Mœnch.

STAPHYLEA

trifolia, L.

ANACARDIACEÆ.

RHUS

aromatica, Ait.
var. trilobata, Gray.
copallina, L.
diversiloba, T. & G.
glabra, L.
Toxicodendron, L.
var. radicans, Torr.
typhina, L.
venenata, DC.

LEGUMINOSÆ.

AMORPHA
canescens, Nutt.
fruticosa, L.
microphylla, Pursh.

AMPHICARPÆA
monoica, Dll.

APIOS
tuberosa, Mœnch.

ASTRAGALUS
aboriginum, Richard.
adsurgens, Pall.
alpinus, L.
Beckwithii, T. & G.
bisulcatus, Gray.
Bourgovii, Gray.
cæspitosus, Gray.
campestris, Gray.
Canadensis, L.
caryocarpus, Ker.
collinus, Dougl,
Cooperi, Gray.
decumbens, Gray.
Drummondii, Dougl.
flexuosus, Dougl.
frigidus, Gray, var. Americanus,
    Watson.
    var. littoralis, Watson.
Gibbsii, Kellog.
glabriusculus, Gray.
Hallii, Gray.
(A. vaginatus, Rich.)
hypoglottis, L.
Kentrophyta, Gray.
lentiginosus, Dougl.
lotiflorus, Hook.
Lyallii, Gray.
microcystis, Gray.
Missouriensis, Nutt.

multiflorus, Gray.
oroboides, Hornem, var. Ameri-
    canus, Gray.
Palliseri, Gray.
pauciflorus, Hook.
pectinatus, Dougl.
polaris, Benth.
Purshii, Dougl.
racemosus, Pursh.
speirocarpus, Gray.
triphyllus, Pursh.

BAPTISIA
leucantha, T. & G.
tinctoria, R. Br.

DESMODIUM
acuminatum, DC.
Canadense, DC.
canescens, DC.
ciliare, DC.
cuspidatum, Hook.
Dillenii, Darlington.
nudiflorum, DC.
paniculatum, DC.
pauciflorum, DC.
rotundifolium, DC.
sessilifolium, T. & G.

GLEDITSCHIA
triacanthos, L.

GLYCYRRHIZA
lepidota, Pursh.
    var. glutinosa, Watson.

GYMNOCLADUS
Canadensis, Lam.

HEDYSARUM
boreale, Nutt.
    var. albiflorum, Macoun.
Mackenzii, Richard.

HOSACKIA

bicolor, Dougl.
decumbens, Benth.
parvifiora, Benth.
Purshiana, Benth,
subpinnata, T. & G.

LATHYRUS

Aphaca, L.
maritimus, Bigel.
ochroleucus, Hook.
Oreganus, Watson.
paluster, L.
   var. myrtifolius, Gray.
pratensis, L.
venosus, Muhl.

LESPEDEZA

capitata, Michx.
hirta, Ell.
repens, Barton.
reticulata, Pers.

LOTUS

corniculatus, Koch.

LUPINUS

arcticus, Watson.
argentus, Pursh, var. argophyllus,
   Watson.
aridus, Dougl. (?)
densiflorus, Benth.
Kingii, Watson.
laxiflorus, Dougl.
lepidus, Dougl.
leucophyllus, Dougl.
littoralis, Dougl.
Lyallii, Gray.
micranthus, Dougl, var. bicolor,
   Watson.
minimus, Dougl.
Nootkatensis, Donn.
   var. Unalaskensis, Watson.
ornatus, Dougl.

perennis, L.
polyphyllus, Lindl.
pusillus, Pursh. (?)
Sabinii, Dougl. (?)
sericeus, Pursh.
sulphureus, Dougl. (?)

MEDICAGO

denticulata, Willd.
lupulina, L.
maculata, Willd.
sativa, L.

MELILOTUS

alba, Lam.
officinalis, Willd.
parviflora, Desf.

ONOBYCHIS

sativa, Lam.

ORNITHOPUS

scorpoides, DC.

OXYTROPIS

arctica, R. Br.
(O. Uralensis, DC., var. pumila,
   Ledeb.)
campestris, L., var. cærulea, Koch,
(O. campestris, DC.)
deflexa, DC.
Lamberti, Pursh.
leucantha, Pers.
Mertensiana, Turcz.
monticola, Gray.
nana, Nutt
nigrescens, Fisch.
   var. arctobia, Gray.
podocarpa, Gray.
splendens, Dougl.
   var. Richardsoni, Hook.
viscida, Nutt.
(O. campestris, DC., var. viscida,
   Watson.

PETALOSTEMON
candidus, Michx.
violaceus, Michx.
    var. pubescens, Gray.

PHASEOLUS
diversifolius, Pers.

PSORALEA
argophylla, Pursh.
esculenta, Pursh.
lanceolata, Pursh.
physodes, Dougl.

ROBINIA
Pseudacacia, L.
viscosa Vent.

SAROTHAMMUS
scoparius, Koch

TEPHROSIA
Virginiana, Pers.

THERMOPSIS
montana, Nutt.
rhombifolia, Richard.

TRIFOLIUM
agrarium, L.
arvense, L.
cyathiferum, Lindl.
depauperatum, Desv.
fucatum, Lindl.
gracilentum, T. & G.
hybridum, L.
involucratum, Willd.
    var. heterodon, Watson.
longipes, Nutt.
medium, L.
megacephalum, Nutt.
microcephalum, Pursh.
microdon, Hook. & Arn.
ornithopodioides, L.

pauciflorum, Nutt.
pratense, L.
procumbens, L.
    var. minus, Koch.
reflexum, L.
repens, L.
resupinatum, L.
tridentatum, Lindl.

TRIGONELLA
corniculata, L.

ULEX
Europæus, L.

VICIA
Americana, Muhl.
    var. linearis, Watson.
    var. truncata, Brewer.
Caroliniana, Walter.
Cracca, L.
hirsuta, Koch.
sativa, L.
    var. angustifolia, Ser.
tetrasperma, Loisel.

ROSACEÆ.

AGRIMONIA
Eupatoria, L.
    var. parviflora, Hook.
parviflora, Ait.

ALCHEMILLA
arvensis, Scop.
vulgaris, L.

AMELANCHIER
alnifolia, Nutt.
Canadensis, T. & G.
    var. (?) oblongifolia, T. & G.
    var. (?) oligocarpa, T. & G.
    var. rotundifolia, T. & G.

CHAMÆRHODOS

erecta, Bunge.
var. Nuttallii, T. & G.

CRATÆGUS

coccinea, L.
Crus-galli, L.
Douglasii, Lindl.
Oxyacantha, L.
rivularis, Nutt.
subvillosa, Schrad.
tomentosa, L.
var. punctata, Gray.
var. pyrifolia, Gray.

DALIBARDA

repens, L.
(Rubus Dalibarda, L.)

DRYAS

octopetala, L.
var. Drummond'i, Watson.
(D. Drummondii, Hook.)
var. integrifolia, Ch. & Sch.

FRAGARIA

Chilensis, Duchesne.
var. Scouleri, Hook.
vesca, L.
Virginiana, Duchesne.

GEUM

album, Gmel.
calthifolium, Menzies.
glaciale, Fisch.
macrophyllum, Willd.
rivale, L.
Rossii, Ser.
var. humile, T. & G.
strictum, Ait.
triflorum, Pursh.
vernum, T. & G.
Virginianum, L.

GILLENIA

trifoliata, Mœnch.

NEILLIA

opulifolia, Benth. & Hook.
var. mollis, Brew. & Wats.

NUTTALIA

cerasiformis, T. & G.

PIRUS

Acuparia, L. (?)
Americana, DC.
arbutifolia, L. f.
var. melanocarpa, Hook.
malus, L.
rivularis, Dougl.
sambucifolia, Cham. & Schl.

POTENTILLA

Anserina, L.
var. grandis, Lehm.
var. Grœnlandica, Tratt.
argentea, L.
arguta, Pursh.
biflora, Willd.
Canadensis, L.
var. simplex, T. & G.
dissecta, Pursh.
var. glaucophylla, Lehm.
var. multisecta, Watson.
var. pinnatisecta, Watson.
effusa, Dougl.
emarginata, Pursh.
fragiformis, Willd.
var. villosa, Reg. & Tiling.
frigida, Villars.
fruticosa, L.
gelida, C. A. Meyer.
glandulosa, Lindl.
gracilis, Dougl.
var. fastigiata, Watson.
var. flabelliformis, T. & G.

var. rigida. Watson.
Hippiana, Lehm.
   var. pulcherrima, Watson.
Hookeriana, Lehm.
humifusa, Nutt.
maculata, Pourret.
nemoralis, Nestler.
nivea, L.
   var. dissecta, Watson.
   var. Vahliana, Seem.
Norvegica, L.
   var. hirsuta, T. & G.
palustris, Scop.
Pennsylvanica, L.
   var. bipinnatifida, T. & G.
   var. glabrata, Watson.
   var. strigosa, Pursh.
pilosa, Willd.
Plattensis, Nutt.
pulchella, R. Br.
rivalis, Nutt. var. millegrana,
   Watson.
supina, L.
tridentata, Sol.

POTERIUM
annuum, Nutt.
Canadense, Benth. & Hook.
officinale, Benth. & Hook.
Sanguisorba, L.
Sitchense, Watson.

PRUNUS
Americana, Marsh.
   var. mollis, T. & G.
demissa, Walp.
emarginata, Walp.
   var. mollis, Brewer.
maritima, Wangenh.
Pennsylvanica, L. f.
pumila, L.
serotina, Ehrh.
Virginiana, L.

PURSHIA
tridentata, DC.

ROSA
acicularis, Lindl.
Arkansana, Porter.
(acicularis, Lindl, Var. Bourgeaniana, Crepin
blanda, Ait.
Californica, Cham. & Schl.
Carolina, L.
Fendleri, Crepin.
   (R parviflora, Ehrh.)
gymnocarpa, Nutt.
humilis, Marsh.
lucida, Ehrh.
micrantha, Smith.
nitida, Willd.
Nutkana, Presl.
pisocarpa, Gray.
pruinosa, Baker.
rubiginosa, L.
Sayi, Schw.
   (R. blanda, Ait. var. setigera,
   Crepin.)
setigera, Michx.
Woodsii, Lindl.

RUBUS
articus, L.
   var. grandiflorus, Ledeb.
Canadensis, L.
Chamæmorus. L.
hispidus, L.
   var. setosus, T. & G.
leucodermis, Dougl.
neglectus, Peck.
Nutkanus, Moc.
nivalis, Dougl.
occidentalis, L.
odoratus, L.
pedatus, Smith.
spectabilis, Pursh.
stellatus, Smith.
strigosus, Michx.
triflorus, Richard.
ursinus, Cham. & Schlecht.
villosus, Ait.

var. frondosus, Torr.
var. humifusus, T. & G.

SIBBALDIA

procumbens, L.

SPIRÆA

Aruncus, L.
betulifolia, Pallas.
var. rosea, Gray.
Douglasii, Hook.
var. Menziesii, Presl.
discolor, Pursh., var. ariæfolia,
Watson.
pectinata, T. & G.
salicifolia, L.
tomentosa, L.

WALDSTEINIA

fragarioides, Tratt.

SAXIFRAGACEÆ.

BOYKINIA

occidentalis, T. & G.
Richardsoni, Gray.

CHRYSOSPLENIUM

alternifolium, L.
Americanum, Schw.

HEUCHERA

Americana, L.
cylindrica, Dougl.
var. alpina, Watson.
(S. Hallii, Gray.)
glabra, Willd.
hispida, Pursh.
micrantha, Dougl
parvifolia, Nutt.

LEPTARRHENA

pyrolifolia, R. Br.

MITELLA

Breweri, Gray.
caulescens, Nutt.
diphylla, L.
nuda, L.
var. (M. prostrata, Michx.)
pentandra, Hook.
trifida, Gray.

PARNASSIA

Caroliniana, Michx.
fimbriata, Koenig.
Kotzebuei, Cham. & Schl
palustris, L.
parviflora, DC.

PHILADELPHUS

Gordonianus, Lindl.
Lewisii, Pursh.

RIBES

aureum, Pursh.
bracteosum, Dougl.
cereum, Dougl.
Cynosbati, L.
divaricatum, Dougl.
var. irriguum, Gray.
floridum, L'Her.
Hudsonianum, Richard.
var. (R. petiolare, Dougl.)
lacustre, Poir.
var. molle, Gray.
var. parvulum, Gray.
laxiflorum, Pursh.
Lobbii, Gray.
oxyacanthoides, L.
prostratum, L'Her.
rotundifolium, Michx.
rubrum, L., var. subglandulosum,
Maxim.
sanguineum, Pursh.
setosum, Lindl.
viscosissimum, Pursh.

SAXIFRAGA
adscendens, L.
azoides, L.
Aizoon, Jacq.
bronchialis, L.
  var. cherlerioides, Engler.
cæspitosa, L.
  var. uniflora, Hook.
cernua, L.
debilis, Engeln.
Eschscholtzii, Sternb.
exilis, Stephan.
flagellaris, Willd.
hieracifolia, Waldst. & Kit.
Hirculus, L.
integrifolia, Hook.
Jamesii, Torr.
leucanthemifolia, Michx., var.
  Brunoniana, T. & G.
  var. ferruginea, T. & G.
Lyallii, Engler.
Mertensiana, Bong.
  (S. heterantha, Hook.)
nivalis, L.
nudicaulis, Don.
occidentalis, Gray.
oppositifolia, L.
Pennsylvanica, L.
punctata, L.
  var. acutidentata, Engler.
ranunculifolia, Hook.
reflexa, Hook.
rivularis, L.
  var. hyperborea, Hook.
  var. Laurentiana, Engler.
serpyllifolia, Pursh.
sileniflora, Sternb.
stellaris, L.
  var. comosa, Poir.
tricuspidata, Retz.
Virginiensis, Michx.

TELLIMA
grandiflora, R. Br.
parviflora, Hook.
tenella, Walp,

TIARELLA
cordifolia, L.
laciniata, Hook.
trifoliata, L.
unifoliata, Hook.

TOLMIEA
Menziesii, T. & G.

CRASSULACEÆ.

PENTHORUM
sedoides, L.

SEDUM
acre, L.
Douglasii, Hook.
obtusatum, Gray.
rhodanthum, Gray.
Rhodiola, DC.
spathulifolium, Hook
stenopetalum, Pursh.
Telephium, L.
ternatum, Michx.

DROSERACEÆ.

DROSERA
Anglica, Hudson.
intermedia, Drev. & Hayne., var.
  Americana, DC.
linearis, Goldie.
rotundifolia, L.

HAMAMELACEÆ.

HAMAMELIS
Virginiana, L.

HALORAGEÆ.

HIPPURIS
maritima, Hellenius.

montana, Ledeb.
vulgaris, L.

MYRIOPHYLLUM

alterniflorum, DC.
heterophyllum, Michx.
spicatum, L.
tenellum, Bigel.
verticillatum, L.

PROSERPINACA

palustris, L.

CALLITRICHACEÆ.

CALLITRICHE

autumnalis, L.
Bolanderi, Heglhim.
verna, L.

MELASTOMACEÆ.

RHEXIA

Virginica, L.

LYTHRACEÆ.

LYTHRUM

alatum, Pursh.
Salicaria, L.

NESÆA
verticillata, HBK.

ONAGRACEÆ.

BOISDUVALIA

densiflora, Watson.
glabella, Walp.

CIRCÆA

alpina, L.
Lutetiana, L.
Pacifica, Asch. & Mag.

CLARKIA

pulchella, Pursh.

EPILOBIUM

affine, Bong.
alpinum, L.
  var. nutans, Lehm.
coloratum, Muhl.
Franciscanum, Barbey.
latifolium, L.
luteum, Pursh.
minutum, Lindl.
  var. folisum, T. & G.
molle, Torr.
Oreganum, Hauskn.
origanifolium, Lam.
palustre, L.
  var. lineare, Gray.
paniculatum, Nutt.
roseum, Schreb.
spicatum, Lam.
  (E. angustifolium, L.)
tetragonum, L.

GAURA

biennis, L.
coccinea, Nutt.

GODETIA

amœna, Lilja.
hispidula, Wat.
epilobioides, Watson.
quadrivulnera, Spach.

LUDWIGIA

alternifolia, L.
palustris, Ell.

ŒNOTHERA

albicaulis, Nutt.
biennis, L.
  var. grandiflora, Lindl.
  var. hirsutissima, Gray.
  var. muricata, Lindl
breviflora, T. & G.
cæspitosa, Nutt.
fruticosa, L.
pumila, L.
(Œ. chrysantha, Mx.)
serrulata, Nutt., var. Douglasii,
  T. & G.
sinuata, L.
strigulosa, T. & G.
  var. pubens, Watson.
triloba, Nutt.

LOASACEÆ.

MENTZELIA

albicaulis, Dougl.
lævicaulis, T. & G.
ornata, T. & G.

CUCURBITACEÆ.

ECHINOCYSTIS

lobata, T. & G.

SICYOS

angulatus, L.

CACTACEÆ.

MAMILLARIA

vivipara, Haworth.

OPUNTIA

fragilis Haworth.
Missouriensis, DC.
Rafinesquii, Engelm.

FICOIDEÆ.

MOLLUGO

verticillata, L.

UMBELLIFERÆ.

ÆTHUSA

Cynapium, L.

ANGELICA

Dawsoni, Watson.
genuflexa, Nutt.
lucida, L.
Lyallii, Watson.

ANTHUSCUS

vulgaris, Pers.

ARCHANGELICA

atropurpurea, Hoffm.
Gmelini, DC.
hirsuta, T. & G.

ARCHEMORA

rigida, DC.

BERULA

angustifolia, Koch.

BUPLEURUM

ranunculoides, L.
rotundifolium, L.

CARUM

Carui, L.
Gairdneri, Benth. & Hook.
Oreganum, Watson.

CAUCALIS
nodosa, Huds.

CHÆROPHYLLUM
procumbens, Crantz.

CICUTA
bulbifera, L.
Californica, Gray.
maculata, L.
virosa, L.

CONIUM
maculatum, L.

CRANTZIA
lineata, Nutt.

CRYPTOTÆNIA
Canadensis, DC.

CYMOPTERUS
glomeratus, Raf.
terebinthinus, T. & G.

DAUCUS
Carota, L.
pusillus, Michx., var. microphyl-
lus, T. & G.

ERIGENIA
bulbosa, Nutt.

FERULA
dissoluta, Watson.
multifida, Gray.

GLYCOSMA
occidentale, Nutt.

HERACLEUM
lanatum, Michx.

HYDROCOTYLE
Americana, L.
prolifera, Kellogg.

LIGUSTICUM
actæifolium, Michx.
apiifolium, Benth. & Hook.
Scoticum, L.

MUSENIUM
divaricatum, Nutt.
var. Hookeri, T. & G.
tenuifolium, Nutt.

ŒNANTHE
sarmentosa, Presl.

OSMORRHIZA
brevistylis, DC.
longistylis, DC.
nuda, Torr.

PEUCEDNAUM
ambiguum, Nutt.
fœniculaceum, Nutt.
leiocarpum, Nutt.
microcarpum, Nutt.
Martindalii, C. & R., var. angus-
tatum, C. & R.
Sandbergii, C. & R.
sativum, Benth. & Hook.
triternatum, Nutt.
utriculatum, Nutt.
villosum, Nutt.

PHELLOPTERUS
littoralis, Schmidt.

PIMPINELLA
integerrima, Benth. & Hook.

SANICULA
arctopoides, Hook. & Arn.
bipinnatifida, Dougl.

Canadensis, L.
Howellii, C. & R.
Marilandica, M.
Menziesii, Hook. & Arn.
Nevadensis, Wat.

SELINUM

Benthami, Watson.
Canadense, Michx.
Dawsoni, C. & R.
Pacificum, Watson.

SIUM

cicutæfolium, Gmel.

THASPIUM

aureum, Nutt.
barbinode, Nutt.
trifoliatum, Gray.

ARALIACEÆ.

ARALIA

hispida, Vent.
nudicaulis, L.
quinquefolia, Dec. & Planch.
racemosa, L.
trifolia, Dec. & Planch.

FATSIA

horrida, Benth. & Hook.

CORNACEÆ.

CORNUS

alternifolia, L. f.
asperifolia, Michx.
Canadensis, L.
circinata, L'Her.
florida, L.
Nuttallii, Audubon.
paniculata, L'Her.
pubescens, Nutt.
sericea, L.
stolonifera, Michx.

Suecica, L.
Unalaskensis, Ledeb.

NYSSA

multiflora, Wangenh.

CAPRIFOLIACEÆ.

ADOXA

Moschatellina, L.

DIERVILLA

trifida, Mœnch.

LINNÆA

borealis, Gronov.
var. longiflora, Torr.

LONICERA

cærulea, L.
var. villosa, T. & G.
ciliata, Muhl.
ciliosa, Poir.
glauca, Hill.
hirsuta, Eaton.
hispidula, Dougl.
var. vacillans, Gray.
involucrata, Banks.
oblongifolia, Hook.
Sullivantii, Gray.
Tartarica, L.
Utahensis, Watson.

SAMBUCUS

Canadensis, L.
glauca, Nutt.
melanocarpa, Gray.
racemosa, L.
var. arborescens, T. & G.

SYMPHORICARPOS

mollis, Nutt.
var. acutus, Gray.
occidentalis, Hook.
racemosus, Michx.
var. pauciflorus, Robbins.

TRIOSTEUM

perfoliatum, L.

VIBURNUM

acerifolium, L.
cassinoides, L.
(S. nudum, L. var. cassinoides,
    T. & G.)
dentatum, L.
lantanoides, Michx.
Lentago, L.
Opulus, L.
pauciflorum, Pylaie.
pubescens, Pursh.

RUBIACEÆ.

GALIUM

Aparine, L.
    var. Vaillantii, Koch.
asprellum, Michx.
boreale, L.
    (G. rubioides, L.)
circæzans, Michx.
Kamtschaticum, Steller.
lanceolatum, Torr.
Mollugo, L.
pilosum, Ait.
tricorne, With.
trifidum, L.
    (var. tinctorium, T. & G.)
    var. bifolium, Macoun.
    var. latifolium, Torr.
    var. pusillum, Gray.
triflorum, Michx.
verum, L.

HOUSTONIA

cærulea, L.
purpurea, L. var. ciliolata, Gray.
    var. longifolia, Gray.

MITCHELLA

repens. L.

SHERARDIA

arvensis, L.

VALERIANACEÆ.

VALERIANA

capitata, Pall.
edulis, Nutt.
Sitchensis, Bong.
    (V. capitata, Willd, var. Hook-
        eri, T. & G.)
sylvatica, Banks.
    (V. dioica, L. var. sylvatica,
        Rich.)
    (V. dioica, L. var. uliginosa,
        T. & G.)

VALERIANELLA

anomala, Gray.
congesta, Lindl.
    (Plectritis, congesta, DC.)
macrocera, Gray.
olitoria, Poll.
    (Fedia olitoria, Vahl.)
samolifolia, Gray.

DIPSACACEÆ.

DIPSACUS

sylvestris, Mill.

COMPOSITÆ.

ACHILLEA

Millefolium, L.
    var. lanata, Koch.
    var. nigrescens, L.
multiflora, Hook.
Ptarmica, L.

ACTINELLA

acaulis, Nutt.
Richardsonii, Nutt.

28

ACTINOMERIS
squarrosa, Nutt.

ADENOCAULON
bicolor, Hook.

AMBROSIA
artemisiæfolia, L.
psilostachya, DC.
trifida, L.
   var. integrifolia, T. & G.

ANAPHALIS
margaritacea, B. & H.

ANTENNARIA
alpina, Gærtn.
Carpathica, R. Br.
   var. pulcherrima, Hook.
dimorpha, T. & G.
dioica, Gærtn.
   var parviflora, T. & G.
   var. rosea, Eaton.
luzuloides, T. & G.
plantaginifolia, Hook.
racemosa, Hook.

ANTHEMIS
arvensis, L.
Cotula, L.
   (Maruta Cotula, DC.)
tinctoria, L.

APARGIDIUM
boreale, T. & G.

APLOPAPPUS
acaulis, Gray.
   (A. acaulis, var. glabratus,
   Eaton.)
Brandegei, Gray.
lanceolatus, T. & G.
   var. Vaseyi, Parry.

Nuttallii, T. & G.
spinulosus, DC.
uniflorus, T. & G.

ARCTIUM
Lappa, L.
   var. minus, Gray.
   var. tomentosum, Gray.

ARNICA
alpina, Olin.
amplexicaulis, Nutt.
Chamissonis, Less.
cordifolia, Hook.
foliosa, Nutt.
latifolia, Bong.
obtusifolia, Less.
Unalaschensis, Less.

ARTEMISIA
borealis, Pall.
   var. Wormskioldii, Bess.
cana, Pursh.
Canadensis, Michx.
caudata, Michx.
discolor, Dougl.
   var. incompta, Gray.
dracunculoides, Pursh.
glauca, Pall.
Lindleyana, Bess.
longifolia, Nutt.
Ludoviciana, Nutt.
tridentata, Nutt.
trifida, Nutt.

ASTER
acuminatus, Michx.
adscendens, Lindl.
alpinus, L.
amplus, Lindl.
angustus, T. & G.
azureus, Lindl.
campestris, Nutt.
canescens, Pursh.
commutatus, Gray.

(A. multiflorus, var. commutatus, T. & G.)
conspicuus, Lindl.
cordifolius, L.
corymbosus, Ait.
diffusus, Ait.
Douglasii, Lindl.
dumosus, L.
Engelmanni, Gray.
ericoides, L.
 var. villosus, T. & G.
falcatus, Lindl.
foliaceus, Lindl.
 var. Eatoni, Gray.
 var. frondeus, Gray.
 var. pubescens, Gray.
Fremonti, Gray.
junceus, Ait.
lævis, L.
linariifolius, L.
Lindleyanus, T. & G.
 var. ciliolatus, Gray.
longifolius, Lam.
macrophyllus, L.
Menziesii, Lindl.
modestus, Lindl.
 (A. mutatus, T. & G.)
 (A. Sayii, Gray.)
multiflorus, Ait.
 var, stricticaulis, T. & G.
nemoralis, Ait.
Novæ-Angliæ, L.
Novi-Belgii, L.
 var. lævigatus, Gray.
 (A. lævigatus, Lam.)
 var. litoreus, Gray.
occidentalis, Nutt.
 var. intermedius, Gray.
Oreganus, Nutt.
 (A. elegans, T. & G.)
paniculatus, Lam.
patens, Ait.
pauciflorus, Nutt.
peregrinus, Pursh.
prenanthoides, Muhl.
ptarmicoides, T. & G.

var. lutescens, Gray.
 (A. lutescens, T. & G.)
puniceus, L.
 var. lævicaulis, Gray.
 (var. firmus, T. & G.)
 var. lucidulus, Gray.
pygmæus, Lindl.
radula, Ait.
 var. strictus, Gray.
radulinus, Gray.
sagittifolius, Willd.
salicifolius, (Lam.?) Ait.
sericeus, Vent.
Sibiricus, L.
 (A. montanus, Rich.)
 var. giganteus, Gray.
spathulatus, Lindl.
subulatus, Michx.
 (A. linifolius, L.)
tanacetifolius, HBK.
tardiflorus. L.
Tradescanti, L. .
umbellatus, Mill.
 var. pubens, Gray.
 var. villosus, Gr.
undulatus, L.
vimineus, Lam.
 var. foliolosus, Gray.

BALSAMORRHIZA

deltoidea, Nutt.
hirsuta, Nutt.
sagittata, Nutt.

BELLIS

perennis, L.

BIDENS

Beckii, Torr.
bullata, L. (?)
cernua, L.
chrysanthemoides, Michx.
connata, Muhl.
frondosa, L.

BIGELOVIA
Douglasii, Gray.
graveolens, Gray.
(B. graveolens, var. hololeuca,
Gray.)

BOLTONIA
latisquama, Gray,

CACALIA
atriplicifolia, L.
tuberosa, Nutt.

CARDUUS
nutans, L.
crispus, L.

CENTAUREA
benedicta, L.
Calcitrapa, L.
Cyanus, L.
Jacea, L.
Melitensis, L.
nigra, L.

CHÆNACTIS
Douglasii, Hook. & Arn.

CHRYSANTHEMUM
arcticum, L.
Balsamita, L.
bipinnatum, L.
integrifolium, Richards,
Leucanthemum, L.
Parthenium, Pers.
segetum, L.

CHRYSOPSIS
villosa, Nutt.
var. hispida, Gray.

CICHORIUM
Intybus, L.

CNICUS
altissimus, Willd., var. discolor,
Gray.
arvensis, Hoffm.
Drummondii, Gray.
var. acaulescens, Gray.
edulis, Gray.
eriocephalus, Gray.
foliosus, Gray.
Hookerianus, Gray.
Kamtschaticus, Maxim.
lanceolatus, Hoffm.
muticus, Pursh.
Pitcheri, Torr.
pumilus, Torr.
undulatus, Gray.

COREOPSIS
discoidea, T. & G.
lanceolata, L.
palmata, Nutt.
tinctoria, Nutt.
trichosperma, Michx., var. tenui-
loba, Gray.
tripteris, L.
verticillata, L.

COTULA
coronopifolia, L.

CREPIS
acuminata, Nutt.
biennis, L.
elegans, Hook.
glauca, T. & G.
intermedia, Gray.
nana, Richards.
occidentalis, Nutt.
var. crinita, Gray.
var. Nevadensis, Kellogg.
runcinata, T. & G.
virens, L.

DYSODIA
chrysanthemoides, Lag.

ECHINACEA
angustifolia, DC.

ERECHTITES
hieracifolia, Raf.

ERIGERON
acris, L.
  (E. alpinus, Linn.)
  var. debilis, Gray.
  var. Drœbachensis, Blytt.
annuus, Pers.
armeriæfolius, Turcz.
Bellidiastrum, Nutt.
bellidifolius, Muhl.
cæspitosus, Nutt.
Canadensis, L.
compositus, Pursh.
  var. discoideus, Gray.
  (var. glabratus, Macoun.)
concinnus, T. & G.
corymbosus, Nutt.
eriocephalus, J. Vahl.
filifolius, Nutt.
flagellaris, Gray.
glabellus, Nutt.
  var. asperus, T. & G.
  var. mollis, Gray.
  var. pubescens, Hook.
grandiflorus, Hook.
hyssopifolius, Michx.
lanatus, Hook.
macranthus, Nutt.
peucephyllus, Gray.
Philadelphicus, L.
poliospermus, Gray.
pumilus, Nutt.
radicatus, Hook.
salsuginosus, Gray.
speciosus, DC.
strigosus, Muhl.
uniflorus, L.

ERIOPHYLLUM
cæspitosum, Dougl.
  var. integrifolium, Gray
  var. leucophyllum, Gray.

EPUATORIUM
ageratoides, L. f.
perfoliatum, L.
purpureum, L.,
  var. maculatum, Darl.
rotundifolium, L.

FRANSERIA
bipinnatifida, Nutt.
Chamissonis, Less.
Hookeriana, Nutt.

GAILLARDIA
aristata, Pursh.

GNAPHALIUM
decurrens, Ives.
microcephalum, Nutt.
Norvegicum' Gunner.
palustre, Nutt.
polycephalum, Michx.
purpureum, L.
Sprengelii, Hook. & Arn.
supinum, Vill.
sylvaticum, L.
uliginosum, L.

GRINDELIA
hirsutula, Hook. & Arn.
integrifolia, DC.
  (G. stricta, DC.)
nana, Nutt.
  var. discoidea, Gray.
squarrosa, Dunal.

GUTIERREZIA
Euthamiæ, T. & G.

HELENIUM
autumnale, L.
  var. grandiflorum, Gray.

HELIANTHUS
annuus, L.

decapetalus, L.
divaricatus, L.
doronicoides, Lam.
giganteus, L.
Maximiliani, Schrad.
Nuttallii, T. & G.
parviflorus, Bernh.
petiolaris, Nutt.
pumilus, Nutt.
rigidus, Desf.
strumosus, L.
tuberosus, L.

HELIOPSIS

lævis, Pers.
scabra, Dunal.

HIERACIUM

albiflorum, Hook.
aurantiacum, L.
Canadense, Michx.
gracile, Hook.
   var. detonsum, Gray.
Gronovii, L.
longipilum, Torr.
murorum, L.
paniculatum, L.
peletarium, Mer.
Pilosella. L.
scabrum, Michx.
Scouleri, Hook.
triste, Cham.
umbellatum, L.
venosum, L.
vulgatum, Fries.

HYMENOPAPPUS

filifolius, Hook.

HYPOCHŒRIS

glabra, L.
radicata, L.

INULA

Helenium, L.

IVA

axillaris, Pursh.
xanthiifolia, Nutt.

JAUMEA

carnosa, Gray.

KRIGIA

amplexicaulis, Nutt.
Virginica, Willd.

LACTUCA

Canadensis, L.
Floridana, Gærtn.
hirsuta, Muhl.
integrifolia, Bigel.
leucophæa, Gray.
pulchella, DC.
Scariola, L.
sativa, L.

LAMPSANA

communis, L.

LAYIA

glandulosa, Hook. & Arn.

LEONTODON

autumnalis, L.
hirtus, L.

LEPACHYS

columnaris, T. & G.
   (Rudbeckia columnaris, Pursh)
   var. pulcherrima, T. & G.

LIATRIS

cylindracea, Michx.
punctata, Hook.
scariosa, Willd.
spictata, Willd.

LUINA
hypoleuca, Benth.

LYGODESMIA
juncea. Don.
rostrata, Gray.

MADIA
filipes, Gray.
glomerata, Hook.
Nuttallii, Gray.
sativa, Molina.
    var. racemosa, Gray.
    (M. dissitiflora, T. & G.)

MATRICARIA
discoidea, DC.
inodora, L.
    var. nana, Hook.

MICROSERIS
Bigelovii, Gray.
nutans. Gray.

MIKANIA
scandens, Gray.

ONOPORDON
acanthium, L.

PETASITES
frigida, Fries.
palmata, Gray.
sagittata, Gray.

PICRIS
echinoides, L.
hieracioides, L., var. Japonica,
    Regel.

POLYMNIA
Canadensis, L.

PRENANTHES
alata, Gray.
    var. sagittata, Gray.
alba, L.
altissima, L.
racemosa. Michx.
serpentaria, Pursh.
    var. nana, Gray.

PSILOCARPHUS
elatior, Gray.
tenellus, Nutt.

RUDBECKIA
hirta, L.
laciniata, L,

SAUSSUREA
alpina, DC.
    var. Ledebouri, Gray.

SENECIO
amplectens, Gray.
aureus, L.
    var. Balsamitæ, T. & G.
    var. borealis, T. & G.
    var. compactus, Gray.
    var. croceus, Gray.
    var. discoideus, Hook.
    var. lanceolatus, Oaks.
    var. obovatus, T. & G.
    var. subnudus, Gray.
canus, Hook.
eremophilus, Richards.
fastigiatus, Nutt.
Fremonti, T. & G.
frigidus, Less,
Hookeri, T. & G.
hydrophilus, Nutt.
integerrimus, Nutt.
Jacobœa, Linn.
lugens, Richards.
    var. exaltatus, Gray.
    var. foliosus, Gray.

megacephalus, Nutt.
palustris, Hook.
petræus, Klatt.
Pseudo-Arnica, Less.
resedifolius, Less.
var. Columbiensis, Gray
sylvaticus, L.
triangularis, Hook.
viscosus, L.
vulgaris, L.

SERICOCARPUS
solidagineus, Nees.

SILPHIUM
perfoliatum, L.
terebinthinaceum, Jacq.

SILYBUM
Marianum, Gœrtn.

SOLIDAGO
arguta, Ait.
bicolor, L.
  var. concolor, T. & G.
  var. lanata, Gray.
cæsia, L.
  var. axillaris. Gray.
Canadensis, L.
  var. procera, T. & G.
  var. scabra, T. & G.
confertiflora, DC.
elongata, Nutt.
Houghtoni, T. & G.
humilis, Pursh.
  var. nana, Gray.
juncea, Ait.
lanceolata, L.
latifolia, L.
lepida, DC.
macrophylla, Pursh.
Missouriensis, Nutt.
  var. montana, Gray.
multiradiata, Ait.
  var. scopulorum, Gray.

neglecta, T. & G.
nemoralis, Ait.
  var. incana, Gray.
occidentalis, Nutt.
odora, Ait.
Ohioensis, Riddell.
patula, Muhl.
puberula, Nutt.
Riddellii, Frank.
rigida, L.
rugosa, Mill.
sempervirens, L.
serotina, Ait.
  var. gigantea, Gray.
speciosa, Nutt.
squarrosa, Muhl.
Terræ-Novæ, T. & G.
uliginosa, Nutt.
Virgaurea, L., var. alpina, Big.

SONCHUS
arvensis, L.
asper, Vill.
oleraceus, L.

STEPHANOMERIA
minor, Nutt.

TANACETUM
Huronense, Nutt.
vulgare, L.

TARAXACUM
officinale, Weber.
  var. alpinum, Koch.
  var. glaucescens. Koch.
  var. lividum, Koch.
  var. scopulorum, Gray.

TETRADYMIA
canescens, DC.

TOWNSENDIA
Parryi, Eaton, var. alpina, Gre
  (T. florifer, Gray.)
sericea, Hook.

TRAGOPOGON
porrifolius, L.
pratensis, L.

TROXIMON
aurantiacum, Hook.
cuspidatum, Pursh.
glaucum, Nutt.
   var. dasycephalum, T. & G.
   var. parviflorum, Gray.
   var. taraxacifolium, Gray.
gracilens, Gray.
grandiflorum, Gray.
heterophyllum, Greene.
humile, Gray.
laciniatum, Gray.

TUSSILAGO
Farfara, L,

VERNONIA
altissima. Nutt.
Noveboracensis, Willd.

WYETHIA
amplexicaulis, Nutt.

XANTHIUM
Canadense, Mill.
   var. echinatum, Gray.
spinosum, L.

LOBELIACEÆ.

LOBELIA
cardinalis, L.
Dortmanna, L.
inflata, L.
Kalmii, L.
spicata, Lam.
   var. hirtella, Gray.
syphilitica, L.

CAMPANULACEÆ.

CAMPANULA.
Americana, L.
aparinoides, Pursh.
lasiocarpa. Cham.
pilosa, Pall.
rapunculoides, L.
rotundifolia, L.
   var. arctica, Lange.
   var. Alaskana, Gray.
Scouleri, Hook.
uniflora, L.

HETEROCODON
rariflorum, Nutt.

SPECULARIA
biflora, Gray.
perfoliata, A. DC.

ERICACEÆ.

ARCTOSTAPHYLOS
alpina, Spreng.
tomentosa, Dougl.
Uva-ursi, Spreng.

ANDROMEDA
ligustrina, Muhl.
polifolia, L.

ALLOTROPA
virgata, T. & G.

ARBUTUS
Menziesii, Pursh.

BRYANTHUS
Aleuticus, Gray.
empetriformis, Gray.
   var. intermedius, Gray.

(B. Grahamii, Hook.)
glanduliflorus, Gray.
taxifolius, Gray.

CALLUNA

vulgaris, Salisb.

CASSANDRA

calyculata, Don.

CASSIOPE

hypnoides, Don.
lycopodioides, Don.
Mertensiana, Don.
Stelleriana, DC.
tetragona, Don.

CHIMAPHILA

maculata, Pursh.
Menziesii, Spreng.
umbellata, Nutt.

CHIOGENES

hispidula, T. & G.

CLADOTHAMNUS

pyrolæflorus, Bong.

EPIGÆA

repens, L.

GAULTHERIA

Myrsinites, Hook.
ovatifolia, Gray.
procumbens, L.
Shallon, Pursh.

GAYLUSSACIA

dumosa, T. & G.
resinosa, T. & G.

KALMIA

angustifolia, L.

glauca, Ait.
   var. microphylla, Hook.
latifolia, L.

LEDUM

glandulosum, Nutt.
latifolium, Ait.
palustre, L.
   var. dilatatum, Wahl.

LOISELEURIA

procumbens, Desv.

MENZIESIA

ferruginea, Smith.
glabella, Gray.

MONESES

uniflora, Gray.

MONOTROPA

fimbriata, Gray.
Hypopitys, L.
   (Hypopitys lanuginosa, Nutt.
uniflora, L.

PTEROSPORA

andromedea, Nutt.

PYROLA

aphylla, Smith.
chlorantha, Swartz.
   var. occidentalis, Gray.
elliptica, Nutt.
minor, L.
picta, Smith.
rotundifolia, L.
   var. asarifolia, Hook.
   var. bracteata, Gray.
   var. incarnata, DC.
   var. pumila, Hook.
   var. uliginosa, Gray.
secunda, L.
   var. pumila, Gray.

RHODODENDRON
albiflorum, Hook.
Californicum, Hook.
(R. macrophyllum, Don.)
Kamtschaticum, Pall.
Lapponicum, Wahl.
maximum, L.
nudiflorum, Torr.
Rhodora, Gmelin.
viscosum, Torr.

VACCINIUM
cæspitosum, Michx.
  var. cuneifolium, Nutt.
Canadense, Kalm.
corymbosum, L.
  var. amœnum, Gray.
  var. atrococcum, Gray.
  var. pallidum, Gray.
macrocarpon, Ait.
  (Oxycoccus macrocarpus
  Pursh.)
myrtilloides, Hook.
  var. rigidum, Hook.
Myrtillus, L.
  var. microphyllum, Hook
occidentale, Gray.
ovalifolium, Smith.
ovatum, Pursh.
Oxycoccus, L.
  (Oxycoccus vulgaris, Pursh.)
  var. intermedium, Gray.
parvifolium, Smith.
Pennsylvanicum, Lam.
  var. augustifolium, Gray.
salicinum, Cham.
stamineum, L.
uliginosum, L.
  var. mucronatum, Herder.
vacillans, Solander.
Vitis-Idæa, L.

DIAPENSIACEÆ.

DIAPENSIA
Lapponica, L.

PLUMBAGINACEÆ.

ARMERIA
vulgaris, Willd.

STATICE
Limonium, L., var. Caroliniana,
Gray.

PRIMULACEÆ.

ANAGALLIS
arvensis, L.

ANDROSACE
Chamæjasme, Host.
occidentalis, Pursh.
septentrionalis, L.

CENTUNCULUS
minimus, L.

DODECATHEON
Media, L.
Jeffreyi, Moore.
Hendersoni, Gray.
frigidum, Cham. & Schl.

DOUGLASIA
arctica, Hook.
nivalis, Lindl.

GLAUX
maritima, L.

LYSIMACHIA
nummularia, L.
punctata, L.
quadrifolia, L.
stricta, Ait,
thyrsiflora, L.

PRIMULA

borealis, Duby.
cuneifolia, Ledeb.
Egaliksensis, Hornem.
farinosa, L.
Mistassinica, Michx.
nivalis, Pall.
officinalis, Linn.
Sibirica, Jacq.
vulgaris, Huds.

SAMOLUS

Valerandi, L., var. Americanus,
Gray.

STEIRONEMA

ciliatum, Raf.
lanceolatum, Gray.
longifolium, Gray.

TRIENTALIS

Americana, Pursh.
Europæa, L.
var. arctica, Ledeb.
var. latifolia, Torr.

OLEACEÆ.

FRAXINUS

Americana, L.
Oregana, Nutt.
pubescens, Lam.
quadrangulata, Michx.
sambucifolia, Lam.
var. Berlandieriana, Gray.

LIGUSTRUM

vulgare, L.

APOCYNACEÆ.

APOCYNUM

androsæmifolium, L.
(var. incanum, A. DC.)

(var. glabrum, Macoun.)
var. pumilum, Gray.
cannabinum, L.
(var. pubescens, Macoun.)
(var. glaberrimum, DC.)
(var. hypericfolium, Gray.)

ASCLEPIADACEÆ.

ACERATES

viridiflora, Ell.
var. lanceolata, Gray.
var. linearis, Gray.

ASCLEPIAS

Cornuti, Decaisne.
incarnata, L.
ovalifolia, Decaisne.
phytolaccoides, Pursh.
purpurascens, L.
quadrifolia, L.
speciosa, Torr.
tuberosa, L.
verticillata, L.

GENTIANACEÆ.

BARTONIA

tenella, Muhl.

FRASERA

Carolinensis, Walt,

GENTIANA

affinis, Griseb.
(G. puberula, Mx.)
alba, Muhl.
Amarella, L., var. acuta, Hk. f
var. stricta, Watson.
var. tenuis, Gray.
Andrewsii, Griseb.
arctophila, Griseb.
aurea, L.

auriculata, Pall.
calycosa, Griseb.
crinita, Frœl.
Douglasiana, Bong.
Forwoodii, Gray.
(G. affinis, Griseb.)
frigida, Hænke.
glauca, Pall.
humilis, Stev.
linearis, Frœl.
  var. lanceolata, Gray.
nivalis, L.
Oregana, Engelm.
platypetala, Griseb.
propinqua, Richards.
prostrata, Hænke.
quinqueflora, Lam.
Saponaria, L.
sceptrum, Griseb.
serrata, Gunner.
tenella, Rottb.
ventricosa, Griseb.

HALENIA

deflexa, Griseb.
  var. Brentoniana, Gray.

LIMNANTHEMUM

lacunosum, Griseb.

MENYANTHES

Crista-galli, Menzies.
trifoliata, L.

PLEUROGYNE

Carinthiaca, Griseb,, var. pusilla,
  Gray.
rotata, Griseb.

SWERTIA

perennis, L., var. obtusa, Griseb.

POLEMONIACÆ.

GILIA

achilleæfolia, Benth.
aggregata, Spreng.
capitata, Dougl.
coronopifolia, Pers.
grandiflora, Gray.
gracilis, Hook.
  (Collomia gracilis, Dougl.)
heterophylla, Dougl.
  (Collomia heterophylla, Hook.)
inconspicua, Dougl.
intertexta, Steud.
linearis, Gray.
  (Collomia linearis, Nutt.)
liniflora, Benth., var. pharna-
  ceoides, Gray.
minutiflora, Benth.
squarrosa, Hook. & Arn.
tenella, Benth.

PHLOX

canescens, T. & G.
divaricata, L.
Douglasii, Hook.
  var. diffusa, Gray.
Hoodii, Richards.
linearifolia, Gray.
longifolia, Nutt.
pilosa, L.
Richardsonii, Hook.
Sibirica, L.
speciosa, Pursh.
subulata, L.

POLEMONIUM

cæruleum, L.
  var. acutiflorum, Ledeb.
confertum, Gray.
humile, Willd.
  var. pulchellum, Gray.
micranthum, Benth.

HYDROPHYLLACEÆ.

ELLISIA
Nyctelea, L.

HYDROPHYLLUM
appendiculatum, Michx.
Canadense L.
capitatum, Dougl.
Virginicum, L.

NEMOPHILA
Menziesii, Hook. & Arn.
parviflora, Dougl.

PHACELIA
circinata, Jacq. f.
Franklinii, Gray.
Menziesii, Torr.
sericea, Gray.
var. Lyallii, Gray.

ROMANZOFFIA
Sitchensis, Bong.
Unalaschkensis, Cham.

BORRAGINACEÆ.

AMSINCKIA
intermedia, Fisch. & Meyer.
lycopsoides, Lehm.
var. bracteosa, Gray.

BORRAGO
officinalis, L.

CYNOGLOSSUM
ciliatum, Dougl.
grande, Dougl.
occidentale, Gray.
officinale, L.
Virginicum, L.

ECHINOSPERMUM
brachycentrum, Ledeb., var.
brachystylum Gray.
deflexum, Lehm, var. Americanum, Gray.
diffusum, Lehm.
floribundum, Lehm.
Lappula, Lehm.
Redowskii, Lehm., var. cupula-
tum, Gray.
var. occidentale, Watson.
Virginicum, Lehm.

ECHIUM
vulgare, L.

HELIOTROPIUM
Curassavicum, L.

KRYNITZKIA *(Eritrichium.)*
Californica, Gray.
Chorisiana, Gray.
circumscissa, Gray.
crassisepala, Gray.
glomerata, Gray.
leiocarpa, Fisch. & Meyer.
leucophæa, Gray.
plebeia, Gray.
Scouleri, Gray.
(Eritrichium fulvum, A. DC.)

LITHOSPERMUM
angustifolium, Michx.
arvense, L.
canescens, Lehm.

hirtum, Lehm.
latifolium, Michx.
officinale, L.
pilosum, Nutt.

LYCOPSIS
arvensis, L.

MERTENSIA
lanceolata, DC.
maritima, Don.
oblongifolia, Don.
paniculata, Don.
Sibirica, Don.
  var. Drummondii, Gray.
Virginica, DC.

MYOSOTIS
arvensis, Hoffm.
laxa, Lehm.
palustris, With.
sylvatica, Hoffm., var. alpestris,
  Koch.
verna, Nutt.
  var. macrosperma, Chapm.

OMPHALODES *(Eritrichium.)*
nana, Gray., var. aretioides, Gray.

ONOSMODIUM
Carolinianum, DC.
  var. molle, Gray.
Virginianum, DC.

PECTOCARYA
penicillata, A. DC.

PLAGIOBOTHRYS
        (Eritrichium.)
tenellus, Gray.
Torreyi, Gray.

SYMPHYTUM
officinale, L.

CONVOLVULACEÆ.

CONVOLVULUS
arvensis, L.
sepium, L., var. Americanus, Sims.
  var. maritima, Macoun.

  var. repens, Gray.
Soldanella, L.
spithamæus, L.

CUSCUTA
arvensis, Beyrich.
compacta, Juss.
epilinum, Weihe.
Gronovii, Willd.
salina, Engelm.
tenuiflora, Engelm.
Trifolii, Bab.

IPOMŒA
pandurata, Meyer.
purqurea, Lam.

SOLANACEÆ.

DATURA
Stramonium, L.
Tatula, L.

HYOSCYAMUS
niger, L.

LYCIUM
vulgare, Dunal.

LYCOPERSICUM
esculentum, Mill.

NICANDRA
physaloides, Gœrtn.

NICOTIANA
attenuata, Torr.
rustica, L.

PETUNIA
parviflora, Juss.

PHYSALIS

grandiflora, Hook.
lanceolata, Michx.
Peruviana, L.
pubescens, L.
Virginiana, Mill.
var. ambigua, Gray.

SOLANUM

Carolinense, L.
Dulcamara, L.
nigrum, L.
rostratum, Dunal.
triflorum, Nutt.

SCROPHULARIACEÆ.

ANTIRRHINUM

Orontium, L.

BARTSIA

alpina, L.
Odontites, Huds.

CASTILLEIA

coccinea, Spreng.
miniata, Dougl.
pallida, Kunth.
    var. septentrionalis, Gray.
parviflora, Bong.
sessiliflora, Pursh.

CHELONE

glabra, L.
nemorosa, Dougl.

COLLINSIA

grandiflora, Dougl.
    var. pusilla, Gray.
parviflora, Dougl.

DIGITALIS

purpurea, L.

EUPHRASIA

officinalis, L.
    var. Tartarica, Benth.

GERARDIA

aspera, Dougl.
flava, L.
pedicularia, L.
purpurea, L.
    var. paupercula, Gray.
quercifolia, Pursh.
tenuifolia, Vahl.
    var. asperula, Gray.

GRATIOLA

aurea, Muhl.
ebracteata, Benth.
Virginiana, L.

ILYSANTHES

gratioloides, Benth.

LIMOSELLA

aquatica, L.
    var. tenuifolia, Hoffm.

LINARIA

Canadensis, Dumont.
Cymbalaria, Mill.
Elatine, Mill.
minor, Desf.
vulgaris, L.

MELAMPYRUM

Americanum, Michx.

MIMULUS

alsinoides, Benth.
floribundus, Dougl.
glabratus, HBK., var. Jamesii,
    Gray.
    (M. Jamesii, T. & G.)
Lewisii, Pursh.
luteus, L.

var. alpinus, Gray.
var. depauperatus, Gray.
moschatus, Dougl.
nasutus, Greene.
ringens, L.

ORTHOCARPUS
attenuatus, Gray.
bracteosus, Benth.
castilleioides, Benth.
hispidus, Benth.
luteus, Nutt.
pusillus, Benth.
tenuifolius, Benth.

PEDICULARIS
bracteosa, Benth.
Canadensis, L.
capitata, Adams.
Chamissonis, Stev.
contorta, Benth.
euphrasioides, Stephan.
flammea, L.
Furbishiæ, Watson.
Grœlandica, Retz.
hirsuta, L.
lanceolata, Michx.
Langsdorffii, Fisch.
var. lanata, Gray.
Lapponica, L.
Menziesii, Benth.
palustris, L., var. Wlassoviana,
Bunge.
pedicellata, Bunge.
racemosa, Dougl.
Sudetica, Willd.
versicolor, Wahl.
verticillata, L.

PENTSTEMON
accuminatus, Dougl.
albidus, Nutt.
(P. cristatus, Nutt.)
confertus, Dougl.
var. cæruleo-purpureus, Gr.

deustus, Dougl.
diffusus, Dougl.
frutescens, Lamb.
glaucus, Graham.
gracilis, Nutt.
humilis, Nutt.
Menziesii, Hook.
var. Scouleri, Gray.
ovatus, Dougl.
pubescens, Solander.
triphyllus, Dougl.
venustus, Dougl.

RHINANTHUS
Crista-galli, L.

SCROPHULARIA
Californica, Cham.
lanceolata, Pursh.
nodosa, L., var. Marilandica,
Gray.

SYNTHYRIS
rubra, Benth.

VERBASCUM
Blattaria, L.
Lychnitis, L.
Thapsus, L.

VERONICA
agrestis, L.
alpina, L.
Americana, Schwein.
Anagallis, L.
arvensis, L.
Buxbaumii, Tenore.
Chamœdrys, L.
Kamtchatica, L. f.
officinalis, L.
peregrina, L.
scutellata, L.
var. pubescens, Macoun.
serpyllifolia, L.
Stelleri, Pall.
Virginica, L.

OROBANCHACEÆ.

APHYLLON
comosum. Gray.
fasciculatum, Gray.
Ludovicianum, Gray.
pinetorum, Gray.
uniflorum, Gray.

BOSCHNIAKIA
glabra, C. A. Meyer.
Hookeri, Walp.

CONOPHOLIS
Americana, Wallr.

EPIPHEGUS
Virginiana, Bart.

LENTIBULARIACEÆ.

PINGUICULA
alpina, L.
villosa, L.
vulgaris, L.

UTRICULARIA
clandestina, Nutt.
cornuta, Michx.
gibba, L.
inflata, Walt.
intermedia, Hayne.
minor, L.
resupinata, B. D. Greene.
vulgaris, L.

BIGNONIACEÆ.

TECOMA
radicans, Juss.

ACANTHACEÆ.

DIANTHERA
Americana, L.

SELAGINACEÆ.

LAGOTIS
glauca, Gærtn.
(Gymnanda Gmelini, Cham. &
Schl.)
(Gymnandra Stelleri, Cham. &
Schl.)

VERBENACEÆ.

PHRYMA
Leptostachya, L.

VERBENA
angustifolia, Michx.
bracteosa, Michx.
hastata, L.
urticæfolia, L.

LABIATEÆ.

AJUGA
reptans, L.

BALLOTA
nigra, L.

BLEPHILIA
hirsuta, Benth.

BRUNELLA
vulgaris, L.

43

CALAMINTHA
clinopodium, Benth.
Nuttallii, Benth.

COLLINSONIA
Canadensis, L.

DRACOCEPHALUM
parviflorum Nutt.

GALEOPSIS
Ladanum, L.
Tetrahit, L.

HEDEOMA
hispida, Pursh.
pulegioides, Pers.

HYSSOPUS
officinalis, L.

ISANTHUS
cæruleus, Michx

LAMIUM
album, L.
amplexicaule, L.
purpureum, L.

LEONURUS
Cardiaca, L.

LOPHANTHUS
anisatus, Benth.
nepetoides, Benth.
scrophulariæfolius, Benth.

LYCOPUS
lucidus, Turcz., var. Americanus, Gray.
sinuatus, Ell.
Virginicus, L.

MARRUBIUM
vulgare, L.

MELISSA
officinalis, L.

MENTHA
aquatica, L.
arvensis, L.
Canadensis, L.
var. glabrata, Benth.
piperita, L.
sativa, L.
viridis, L.

MICROMERIA
Douglasii, Benth.

MONARDA
clinopodia, L.
didyma, L.
fistulosa, L.
var. mollis, Benth.
punctata, L.

NEPETA
Cataria, L.
Glechoma, Benth.

ORIGANUM
vulgare, L.

PHYSOSTEGIA
parviflora, Nutt.
Virginiana, Benth.

PYCNANTHEMUM
incanum, Michx.
lanceolatum, Pursh.
muticum, Pers., var. pilosum, Gray.

SATUREIA
hortensis, L.

SCUTELLARIA
angustifolia, Pursh.
canescens, Nutt.
galericulata, L.
lateriflora, L.
parvula, Michx.

STACHYS
aspera, Michx.
ciliata, Dougl.
   var. pubens, Gray.
palustris, L.

TEUCRIUM
Botrys, L,
Canadense, L.
occidentale, Gray.

THYMUS
Serpyllum, L.

PLANTAGINACEÆ.

LITTORELLA
lacustris, L.

PLANTAGO
Bigelovii, Gray.
cordata, Lam.
decipiens, Barneoud.
eriopoda, Torr.
lanceolata. L.
macrocarpa, Cham. & Schl.
major, L.
   var. Asiatica, Decaisne.
   var. bracteata, Macoun.
   var. minima, Decaisne.
maritima, L.
media, L.
Patagonica, Jacq., var. aristata,
   Gray.

var. gnaphalioides, Gray.
var. spinulosa, Gray.
pusilla, Nutt.
Rugelii, Decaisne.

NYCTAGINACEÆ.

ABRONIA
latifolia, Esch.
umbellata, Lam.

OXYBAPHUS
angustifolius, Sweet.
hirsutus, Sweet.
nyctagineus, Sweet.

AMARANTACEÆ.

ACNIDA
ruscocarpa, Michx.
tuberculata. Gray.

AMARANTUS
albus, L.
blitoides, Watson.
hypochondriacus, L.
paniculatus, L.
retroflexus, L.

CHENOPODIACEÆ.

ATRIPLEX
Alaskensis, Watson.
arenaria, Nutt.
argentea, Nutt.
Endolepis, Watson.
Gmelini, C. A. Meyer.
Nuttallii, Watson.
patula, L., var. hastata, Gray.
   var. littoralis, Gray.
   var. subspictata, Watson.
rosea, L.
zosteræfolia, Watson.

AXYRIS
amarantioides, L.

CHENOPODIUM
album, L.
   var. viride.
ambrosioides, L.
   var. anthelminticum, Gray.
Bonus-Henricus, L.
Botrys, L.
capitatum, Watson.
Fremonti, Watson.
glaucum, L.
humile, Hook.
   (C. rubrum, L., var. humile,
   Moq.)
hybridum, L.
leptophyllum, Nutt.
   var. subglabrum, Watson.
rubrum, L.
urbicum, L.

CORISPERMUM
hyssopifolium, L.

CYCLOLOMA
platyphyllum, Moq.

EUROTIA
lanata, Moq.

KOCHIA
scoparia, L.

MONOLEPIS
chenopodioides, Moq.

SALICORNIA
ambigua, Michx.
herbac a, L.
mucronata, Bigel.

SALSOLA
Kali, L.

SARCOBATUS
vermiculatus, Torr.

SUÆDA
depressa, Watson.
   var. erecta, Watson.
linearis, Torr., var. ramosa,
   Watson.

PHYTOLACCACEÆ.

PHYTOLACCA
decandra, L.

POLYGONACEÆ.

ERIOGONUM
androsaceum, Benth.
flavum, Nutt.
heracleoides, Nutt.
multiceps, Nees.
ovalifolium, Nutt.
umbellatum, Torr.

FAGOPYRUM
esculentum, Mœnch.

KOENIGIA
Islandica, L.

OXYRIA
digyna, Campdera.

POLYGONUM
acre, HBK.
amphibium, L.
arifolium, L.
articulatum, L.
aviculare, L.
Bistorta, L.
Careyi, Olney.
cilinode, Michx.

coarctatum, Dougl.
Convolvulus, L.
dumetorum, L., var. scandens,
   Gray.
erectum, L.
Hartwrightii, Gray.
Hydropiper, L.
hydropiperoides, Michx.
imbricatum, Nutt.
incarnatum, Ell.
intermedium, Nutt.
lapathifolium, Ait.
maritimum, L.
minimum, Watson.
Muhlenbergii, Watson.
nodosum, Pers.
orientale, L.
Paronychia, Cham. & Schl.
Pennsylvanicum, L.
Persicaria, L.
polymorphum, Ledeb
ramosissimum, Michx.
sagittatum, L.
Tartaricum, L.
tenue, Michx.
  var. latifolium, Engelm.
Virginianum, L.
viviparum, L.

RUMEX

Acetosa, L.
Acetosella, L.
Britannicus, L.
  (R. orbiculatus, Gray.)
crispus, L.
maritimus, L.
obtusifolius, L.
occidentalis, Watson.
Patientia, L.
paucifolius, Nutt.
salicifolius, Weinm.
sanguineus, L.
venosus, Pursh.
verticillatus, L.

ARISTOLOCHIACEÆ.

ASARUM
Canadense, L.
caudatum, Lindl.

PIPERACEÆ.

SAURURUS
cernuus, L.

LAURACEÆ.

LINDERA
Benzoin, Meisn.

SASSAFRAS
officinale, Nees.

THYMELEACEÆ.

DAPHNE
Mezereum, L.

DIRCA
palustris, L.

ELÆAGNACEÆ.

ELÆAGNUS
argentea, Pursh.

SHEPHERDIA
argentea, Nutt.
Canadensis, Nutt.

LORANTHACEÆ.

ARCEUTHOBIUM
Americanum, Nutt.
robustum, Engelm.
vaginatum, Eichler.

SANTALACEÆ.

COMANDRA
livida, Richards.
pallida, A. DC.
umbellata, Nutt.

EUPHORBIACEÆ.

ACALYPHA
Virginica, L.

EUPHORBIA
commutata, Engelm.
corollata, L.
Cyparissias, L.
glyptosperma, Engelm.
Helioscopia, L.
hypericifolia, L.
maculata, L.
obtusata, Pursh.
Peplus, L.
platyphylla, L.
polygonifolia, L.
serpens, HBK.
serpyllifolia, Pers.

MERCURIALIS
annua, L.

URTICACEÆ.

BŒHMERIA
cylindrica, Willd.

CANNABIS
sativa, L.

CELTIS
occidentalis, L.

HUMULUS
Lupulus, L.

LAPORTEA
Canadensis, Gaudich.

MORUS
alba, L.
rubra, L.

PARIETARIA
Pennsylvanica, Muhl.

PILEA
pumila, Gray.

ULMUS
Americana, L.
fulva, Michx.
racemosa, Thomas.

URTICA
dioica, L.
gracilis, Ait.
holosericea, Nutt.
Lyallii, Watson.
urens, L.

PLATANACEÆ.

PLATANUS
occidentalis, L.

JUGLANDACEÆ.

CARYA
alba, Nutt.
amara, Nutt.
porcina, Nutt.
tomentosa, Nutt.

JUGLANS
cinerea, L.
nigra, L.

MYRICACEÆ.

MYRICA
asplenifolia, Endl.
Californica, Cham.
cerifera, L.
Gale, L.

BETULACEÆ.

ALNUS
incanus, Willd.
    var. virescens, Watson.
rhombifolia, Nutt.
rubra, Bong.
viridis, DC.

BETULA
alba, var. populifolia, Spach.
glandulosa, Michx.
lenta, L.
lutea, Michx. f.
nigra, L.
occidentalis, Hook.
papyrifera, Michx.
pumila, L.

CUPULIFERÆ.

CARPINUS
Caroliniana, Walt.

CASTANEA
vesca, L,. var. Americana, Mx.

CORYLUS
Americana, Walt.
rostrata, Ait.
    var. Californica, A. DC.

FAGUS
ferruginea, Ait.

OSTRYA
Virginica, Willd.

QUERCUS
alba, L.
bicolor, Willd.
coccinea, Willd.
Garryana, Dougl.
macrocarpa, Michx.
obtusiloba, Michx.
palustris, Du Roi.
prinoides, Willd.
Prinus, L.
rubra, L.
tinctoria, Bartr.

SALICACEÆ.

POPULUS
angustifolia, James.
balsamifera, L.
    var. candicans, Gray.
grandidentata, Michx.
monilifera, Ait.
tremuloides, Michx.
trichocarpa, T. & G.

SALIX
adenophylla, Hook.
alba, L., var. cœrulea, Koch.
amygdaloides, And.
arctica, Pall.
    var. petræa, And.
argyrocarpa, And.
balsamifera, Barratt.
Barclayi, And.
    var. latiuscula, Aud.
Barrattiana, Hook.
candida, Willd.
Chamissonis, And.
chlorophylla, And.
cordata, Muhl.
    var. angustata, And.
    var. Mackenziana, Hook.

desertorum Rich.
discolor, Muhl.
    var. eriocephala, And.
Drummondiana, Barratt.
flavescens, Nutt.
    var. Scouleriana, Bebb.
    var. tenuijulis, And.
fulcrata, var. subglauca, And.
glauca, L.
    var. villosa, And.
glaucophylla, Bebb.
herbacea, L.
Hookeriana, Barratt.
humilima, And.
humilis, Muhl.
lanata, L.
    var. Macouniana, Bebb. N. var.
lasiandra, Benth.
    var. lancifolia Bebb.
longifolia, Muhl.
    var. argyrophylla, And.
lucida, Muhl.
macrocarpa, Nutt.
myrtilloides, L.
nigra, Marsh.
Novæ-Angliæ, And.,var. myrtilli-
    folia, And.
    var. pseudo-cordata, And.
    var. pseudo-myrsinites, And.
orbicularis, And.
ovalifolia, Traut.
Pallasii, Anders., var. crassijulis,
    Anders.
    var. diplodyctya, Anders.
petiolaris, Smith.
    var. gracilis, And.
phlebophylla, And.
phylicoides, And.
polaris, Wahl.
prolixa, And.
reticulata, L.
    var. nivalis, And.
Richardsoniana, Hook.
rostrata, Rich.
sericea, Marsh.
sessilifolia, Nutt.

Sitchensis, Sanson.
    var. angustifolia, Bebb.
speciosa, Hook. & Arn.
tristis, Ait.
Uva-ursi, Pursh.
vestita, Pursh.
viminalis, L.

EMPETRACEÆ.

COREMA
Conradii, Torr.

EMPETRUM
nigrum, L.

CERATOPHYLLACEÆ.

CERATOPHYLLUM
demersum, L.

CONIFERÆ.

ABIES
amabilis, Forbes.
balsamea, Marshall.
grandis, Lindl.
subalpina, Engelm.

JUNIPERUS
communis, L.
    var. alpina, Gaud.
occidentalis, Hook.
Sabina, L., var. procumbens, Ph.
Virginiana, L.

LARIX
Americana, Michx.
Lyallii, Parlat.
occidentalis, Nutt.

PICEA

alba, Link.
Engelmanni, Engelm.
nigra, L.
Sitchensis, Carr.

PINUS

albicaulis, Engelm.
Banksiana, Lambert.
contorta, Dougl.
flexilis, James.
monticola, Dougl.
Murrayana, Balf.
ponderosa, Dougl., var. scopulorum, Engelm.
resinosa, Ait.
rigida, Mill.
Strobus, L.

PSEUDOTSUGA

Douglasii, Carr.

TAXUS

baccata, L., var. Canadensis, Gray.
brevifolia, Nutt.

THUYA

excelsa, Bong.
gigantea, Nutt.
occidentalis, L.
sphæroidea, Spreng.

TSUGA

Canadensis, Carr.
Mertensiana, Carr.
Pattoniana, Engelm.

HYDROCHARIDACEÆ.

ELODEA

Canadense, Planch.

VALLISNERIA

spiralis, L.

ORCHIDACEÆ.

APLECTRUM

hiemale, Nutt.

ARETHUSA

bulbosa, L.

CALOPOGON

pulchellus, R. Br.

CALYPSO

borealis, Salisb.

CORALLORHIZA

innata, R. Br.
Mertensiana, Bong.
multiflora, Nutt.
odontorhiza, Nutt.
striata, Lindl.

CYPRIPEDIUM

acaule, Ait.
arietinum, R. Br.
montanum, Dougl.
parviflorum, Salisb.
passerinum, Rich.
pubescens, Willd.
spectabile, Swartz.

EPIPACTIS

gigantea, Dougl.

GOODYERA

Menziesii, Lindl.
pubescens, R. Br.
repens, R. Br.

HABENARIA

blephariglottis, Hook.
bracteata, R. Br.
ciliaris, R. Br.
dilatata, Gray.
elegans, Bolander.
fimbriata, R. Br.
gracilis, Watson.
Hookeri, Torr.
   var. oblongifolia, Paine.
hyperborea, R. Br.
lacera, R. Br.
leucophæa, Gray.
leucostachys, Watson.
Menziesii, Lindl.
obtusata, Richards.
orbiculata, Torr.
psycodes, Gray.
sparsiflora, Watson.
tridentata, Gray.
Unalaschensis, Watson.
virescens, Spreng.

LIPARIS

Lœselii, Richards.

LISTERA

convallarioides, Nutt.
cordata, R. Br.

MICROSTYLIS

monophyllos, Lindl.
ophioglossoides, Nutt.

ORCHIS

rotundifolia, Pursh.
spectabilis, L.

POGONIA

ophioglossoides, Nutt.
pendula, Lindl.
verticillata, Nutt.

SPIRANTHES

cernua, Richard.
gracilis, Bigel.
latifolia, Torr.
Romanzoffiana, Cham.

HÆMODORACEÆ.

ALETRIS

farinosa, L.

IRIDACEÆ.

IRIS

Hookeri, Penny.
lacustris, Nutt.
tenax, Dougl.
versicolor, L.
Virginica, L.

SISYRINCHIUM

anceps, L.
Californicum, Ait. f.
grandiflorum, Dougl.
mucronatum, Michx.

AMARYLLIDACEÆ.

HYPOXIS

erecta, L.

DIOSCOREACEÆ.

DIOSCOREA

villosa, Torr.

LILIACEÆ.

ALLIUM

acuminatum, Hook.
Canadense, Kalm.

cernuum, Roth.
Geyeri, Watson.
Nevii, Watson.
reticulatum, Fras.
Schœnoprasum, L,
stellatum, Fras.
tricoccum, Ait.
Vancouverense, Macoun.

ASPARAGUS
officinalis, L.

BRODIÆA
Douglasii, Watson.
grandiflora, Smith.
lactea, Watson.

CALOCHORTUS
elegans, Pursh., var. nanus,
Wood.
macrocarpus, Dougl.

CAMASSIA
esculenta, Lindl.
Fraseri, Torr.
Leichtlinii, Watson.

CHAMÆLIRIUM
Carolinianum, Willd.

CLINTONIA
borealis, Raf.
uniflora, Kunth.

ERYTHRONIUM
albidum, Nutt.
Americanum, Smith.
grandiflorum, Pursh.
var. (?) albiflorum, Hook.
var. (?) minus, Morren.
var. giganteum, Hook.
var. (?) Smithii, Hook.
propullans, Gray.

FRITILLARIA
Kamtschatcensis, Ker.
lanceolata, Pursh.
var. floribunda, Benth.
var. gracilis, Watson.
pudica, Spreng.

HEMEROCALLIS
fulva, L.

LILIUM
Canadense, L.
Carolinianum, Michx..
Columbianum, Hanson.
Philadelphicum, L.

LLOYDIA
serotina, Reich.

MAIANTHEMUM
bifolium, DC., var. dilatatum,
Wood.
Canadense, Desf,

MEDEOLA
Virginiana, L.

MELANTHIUM
Virginicum, L.

POLYGONATUM
biflorum, L.
giganteum, Deitr.

PROSARTES
Hookeri, Torr.
lanuginosa, Don.
Menziesii, Don.
Oregana, Watson.
trachycarpa. Watson.

SMILACINA
amplexicaulis, Nutt.
racemosa, Desf.
sessilifolia, Nutt.
stellata, Desf.
trifolia, Desf.

SMILAX
herbacea, L
hispida, Muhl.
quadrangularis, Pursh.

STENANTHIUM
occidentale, Gray.

SIREPTOPUS
amplexifolius, DC.
roseus, Michx.

TOFIELDIA
borealis, Wahl.
coccinea, Richards.
  var. major, Hook.
glutinosa, Willd.
occidentalis, Watson.

TRILLIUM
cernuum, L.
erectum, L., var. atropurpureum.
  Hook.
  var. album, Pursh.
  var. declinatum, Gray.
  vaa. ochroleucum, Hook.
erythrocarpum, Michx.
grandiflorum, Salisb.
ovatum, Pursh.

UVULARIA
grandiflora, Smith.
perfoliata, L
sessilifolia, L.

VERATRUM
viride, Ait.

XEROPHYLLUM
tenax, Nutt.

ZYGADENUS
elegans, Pursh.
paniculatus, Watson.
venenosus, Watson.

PONTEDERIACEÆ.

HETERANTHERA
graminea, Vahl.

PONTEDERIA
cordata, L.
  var. angustifolia, Gray.

XYRIDACEÆ

XYRIS
flexuosa, Muhl., var. pusilla, Gray.

JUNACEÆ.

JUNCUS
acuminatus, Michx., var. legitimus, Engelm.
alpinus, Vill., var. insignis, Fr.
arcticus, Willd.
  var. Sitchensis, Engelm.
articulatus, L.
Balticus, Dethard, var. littoralis,
  Engelm.
  var. montanus, Engelm.
biglumis, L.
bufonius, L.
  var. fasciculiflorus, Boiss.
Canadensis, J. Gay, var. coarctatus, Engelm.
  var. longecaudatus, Eng.
castaneus. Smith.
Drummondii, Meyer.

effusus, L.
var. brunneus, Engelm.
var. conglomeratus, Gray.
falcatus, E. Meyer.
filiformis, L.
Gerardi, Lois.
Greenei, Oakes & Tuckerm.
Lescurii, Bolander.
longistylis, Torr.
marginatus, Rostk., var. pauci-
    capitatus, Engelm.
var. vulgaris. Engelm.
Mertensianus, Bong.
var paniculatus, Engelm.
militaris, Bigel.
Nevadensis, Watson.
nodosus, L., var. genuinus,
    Engelm.
var. megacephalus, Torr.
Parryi, Engelm.
pelocarpus, E. Meyer.
var. (?) subtilis, Engelm.
stygius, L.
supiniformis, Engelm.
tenuis, Willd.
var. congestus, Engelm.
var. secundus, Engelm.
trifidus, L.
triglumis, L.
Vaseyi, Engelm.
xiphioides, E. Mey., var. littoralis,
    Engelm.
var. macranthus, Engelm.
var. montanus, Engelm.
var. triandrus, Engelm.

LUZULA

arcuata, Meyer.
campestris, Desv., var. comosa,
    Hook.
var. pallescens, Hook.
var. vulgaris, Hook.
comosa, Meyer.
var. congesta, Watson.
var. macrantha, Watson.
var. subsessilis, Watson.

divaricata, Watson.
hyperborea, R. Br., var. major,
    Hook.
var. minor, Hook.
pilosa, Willd.
spadicea, DC., var. melanocarpa,
    Meyer.
var. parviflora, Meyer.
var. subcongesta, Meyer.
spicata, Desv.

TYPHACEÆ.

SPARGANIUM

affine, Schnitz.
androcladum, Morong.
eurycarpum, Engelm.
hyperboreum, Læst., var. Ameri-
    canum, Beeby.
minimum, Bauhin.
simplex, Huds.

TYPHA

angustifolia, L.
latifolia, L.

ARACEÆ.

ACORUS

Calamus, L.

ARISÆMA

Dracontium, Schott.
triphyllum. Torr.

CALLA

palustris, L,

LYSICHITON

Kamtschatcense, Schott.

PELTANDRA

Virginica, Raf.

SYMPLOCARPUS
foetidus, Salisb.

LEMNACEÆ.

LEMNA
minor, L.
polyrrhiza, L.
trisulca, L.

WOLFFIA
Brasiliensis, Weddell.
Columbiana, Karsten.

ALISMACEÆ.

ALISMA
Plantago, L., var. Americanum,
Gray.

DAMASONIUM
Californicum, Torr.

ECHINODORUS
parvulus, Engelm.

SAGITTARIA
calycina, Eng., var. spongiosa,
Engelm.
graminea, Pursh.
heterophylla, Pursh.
var. rigida, Engelm.
variabilis, Eng., var. angustifolia,
Engelm.
var. diversifolia, Engelm.
var. gracilis, Engelm.
var. hastata, Engelm.
var. latifolia, Engelm.
var. obtusa, Engelm.
var. pubescens, Engelm.

NAIADACEÆ.

LILÆA
subulata, HBK.

NAIAS
flexilis, Rostk. & Schmidt.
var. robusta, Morong.

PHYLLOSPADIX
Scouleri, Hook.

POTAMOGETON
amplifolius, Tuckerm.
Claytonii, Tuckerm.
gramineus, L.
var. graminifolius, Fries.
var. heterophyllus, Fries.
var. maximus, Morong.
hybridus, Michx.
lonchites, Tuckerm.
lucens, L.
marinus, L.
var. Macounii, Morong.
mucronatus, Schrad.
natans, L.
var. prolixus, Koch.
Oakesianus, Robbins.
obtusifolius, M. & K.
pauciflorus, Pursh.
var. Niagarensis, Gray.
pectinatus, L.
perfoliatus, L.
var. lanceolatus, Robbins.
prælongus, Wulf.
pusillus, L.
var. panormitanus, Biv.
var. vulgaris, Fries.
Robbinsii, Oakes.
rufescens, Schrad.
rutilans, Wolfgang.
Spirillus, Tuckerm.
Vaseyi, Robbins.
Zizii, M. & K.
zosterifolius, Schum.

RUPPIA
maritima, L.

SCHEUCHZERIA
palustris, L.

TRIGLOCHIN
maritimum, L.
  var. elatum, Gray.
palustre, L.

ZANNICHELLIA
palustris, L.

ZOSTERA
marina, L.

ERIOCAULONACEÆ.

ERIOCAULON
septangulare, With.

CYPERACEÆ.

CAREX
albata, Bailey.
acuta, L.
  var. prolixa, Hornem.
adusta, Boott.
Alascana, Bœckl.
alopecoidea, Tuckerm.
alpina, Swartz.
ambusta, Boott.
aquatilis, Wahl.
  var. epigeios, Læst.
arcta, Boott.
arctata, Boott.
  var. Faxoni, Bailey.
arida, Schw. & Torr.
Assiniboinensis, W. Boott.
athrostachya, Olney.
atrata, L.
  var. nigra. Boott.
  var. ovata, Boott.
atrofusca, Schk.
aurea, Nutt.

Backii, Boott.
Barbaræ, Dew.
bicolor, All.
brizoides, L., var. nemoralis, Wimm.
bromoides, Schk.
Brongniartii, Kunth., var. densa, Bailey.
Buxbaumii, Wahl.
cæspitosa, L.
  var. filifolia, Boott.
canescens, L.
  var. alpicola, Wahl.
  var. vulgaris, Bailey.
capillaris, L.
capitata, L.
  var. Krausei, Krantz.
cephaloidea, Boott.
cephalophora, Muhl.
  var. angustifolia, Boott.
chordorhiza, Ehrh.
circinata, Meyer.
compacta, R. Br.
concinna, R. Br.
conoidea, Schk.
Crawei, Dew.
crinita, Lam.
  var. gynandra, Sch. & Torr.
cryptocarpa, Meyer.
debilis, Michx.
decidua, Boott.
Deweyana, Schw.
  var. Bolanderi, W. Boott.
  var. sparsiflora, Bailey.
digitalis, Willd.
dioica, L.
disticha, Huds.
Douglasii, Boott.
eburnea, Boott.
echinata, Murr.
  var. conferta, Bailey.
  var. microstachys, Bœkl.
Emmonsii, Dew.
exilis, Dew.
festiva, Dew.
  var. gracilis, Olney

59

var. Haydeniana, W. Boott.
filifolia, Nutt.
filiformis, L.
flava, L.
var. rectorostrata, Bailey.
flexilis, Rudge.
folliculata, L.
formosa, Dew.
Franklinii, Boott.
fulva, Good. (?)
Gayana. Desv.
Geyeri, Boott.
glareosa, Wahl.
glauca, Scop.
Gmelini, Hook.
gracillima, Schw.
granularis, Muhl.
Grayii, Carey.
grisea, Wahl.
gynocrates, Wormsk.
heleonastes, Ehrh.
Hendersoni, Bailey.
heteroneura, W. Boott.
Hitchcockiana, Dew.
Hoodii, Boott.
Houghtonii, Torr.
hystricina, Willd.
incurva, Lightf.
intumescens, Rudge.
invisa, Bailey.
Jamesii, Torr.
lagopina, Wahl.
lanuginosa, Michx.
var. æmathorhyncha.
laxiflora, Lam.
var. intermedia, Boott.
var. latifolia, Boott.
var. patulifolia, Carey.
var. striatula, Carey.
leiocarpa, Meyer.
leiorhyncha, Meyer.
lenticularis, Michx.
leporina, L., var. Americana,
Olney.
Liddoni, Boott.
limosa, L.

var. stygia, Bailey.
livida, Willd.
longirostris, Torr.
lurida, Wahl.
var. divergens, Bailey.
var. polystachya, Bailey.
Lyoni, Boott.
macrocephala, Willd.
Magellanica, Lam.
marcida, Boott.
maritima, Muller.
Meadii, Dew.
melanocarpa, Cham.
Mertensii, Presc.
Michauxiana, Bœckl.
microglochin, Wahl.
miliaris, Michx.
misandra, R. Br.
monile, Tuckerm.
Muhlenbergii, Schk.
muricata, L., var. confixa, Bailey.
var. gracilis, Boott.
nardina, Fries.
nigricans, Meyer.
Norvegica, Schk.
Novæ-Angliæ, Schw.
var. deflexa, Bailey.
var. Rossii, Bailey.
obesa, All., var. minor, Boott.
obtusata, Lilj.
Œderi, Retz.
oligocarpa, Schk.
oligosperma, Michx.
pallescens, L.
punicea, L.
Parryana, Dew.
pauciflora, Lightf.
pedunculata, Muhl.
Pennsylvanica, Lam.
petricosa, Dew.
physocarpa, Presl.
pinguis, Bailey.
plantaginea, Lam.
platyphylla, Carey.
podocarpa, R. Br.
polytrichoides, Muhl.

prasina, Wahl.
pratensis, Drej.
Pseudo-Cyperus, L.
 var. comosa, W. Boott.
pubescens, Muhl.
Pyrenaica, Wahl.
Raeana, Boott.
rariflora, Smith.
Raynoldsii, Dew.
remota, L.
retrocurva, Dew.
retrorsa, Schw.
 var. Hartii, Carey.
Richardsonii, R. Br.
riparia, Curtis.
rosea, Schk.
 var. radiata, Dew.
 var. retroflexa, Torr.
rostrata, With.
 var. utriculata, Bailey.
rotundata, Wahl.
rupestris, All.
salina, Wahl.
 var. mutica, Wahl.
 var. (?) robusta, Bailey.
Saskatschewana, Bœckl.
saxatilis, L.
 var. Grahami, Hook. & Arn.
scabrata, Schw.
Schweinitzii, Dew.
scirpoidea, Michx.
scoparia, Schk.
siccata, Dew.
Sitchensis, Presc.
sparganioides, Muhl.
squarrosa, L.
stenophylla, Wahl,
Steudelii, Kunth.
stipata, Muhl.
straminea, Schk.
 var. alata, Bailey.
 var. aperta, Boott.
 var. festucacea, Boott.
 var. fœnea, Torr.
 var. mixta, Bailey.
 var. moniliformis, Tuckerm.

 var. tenera, Boott.
stricta, Lam.
 var. decora, Bailey.
stylosa, Meyer.
subspathacea, Wormsk.
subulata, Michx.
sychnocephala, Carey.
tenella, Schk.
tentaculata, Muhl.
tenuiflora, Wahl.
teretiuscula, Good.
 var. ramosa, Boott.
tetanica, Schk.
Tolmiei, Boott.
Torreyi, Tuckerm.
torta, Boott.
tribuloides, Wahl.
 var. cristata, Bailey.
 var. reducta, Bailey.
triceps, Michx.
trichocarpa, Muhl.
 var. aristata, Bailey.
 var. Deweyi, Bailey.
trisperma, Dew.
Tuckermani, Boott.
umbellata, Schk.
 var. brevirostris, Boott.
ursina, Dew.
vaginata, Tausch.
varia, Muhl.
vesicaria, L.
 var. major, Boott.
virescens, Muhl.
vulgaris, Fries.
 var. alpina, Boott.
 var. hyperborea, Boott.
 var. juncella, Fries.
vulpinoidea, Michx.
Willdenovii, Schk.

CLADIUM
 mariscoides, Torr.

CYPERUS
 aristatus Rottb.
 diandrus, Torr.

var. castaneus, Torr.
erythrorhizos, Muhl.
esculentus, L.
filiculmis, Vahl.
flavescens, L.
Schweinitzii, Torr.
strigosus, L.

DULICHIUM

spathaceum, Pers.

ELEOCHARIS

acicularis, R. Br.
compressa, Sulliv.
intermedia, Schultes.
obtusa, Schultes.
palustris, R. Br.
 var. calva, Gray.
 var. glaucescens, Gray.
pauciflora, Watson.
pygmæa, Torr.
Robbinsii, Oakes.
 var. occidentalis, Watson.
tenuis, Schultes.

ERIOPHORUM

alpinum, L.
capitatum, Host.
cyperinum, L.
 var. laxus, Gray.
gracile, Koch.
 var. paucinervium, Engelm.
lineatum, B. & H.
polystachyon, L.
 var. angustifolium, Gray.
russeolum, Fries.
vaginatum, L.
Virginicum, L.
 var. album, Gray.

KOBRESIA

caricina, Willd.
scirpina, Willd.

RHYNCHOSPORA

alba, Vahl.
capillacea, Torr.
fusca, R. & S.
glomerata, Vahl

SCIRPUS

atrovirens, Muhl.
cæspitosus, L.
Clintonii, Gray.
fluviatilis, Gray.
lacustris, L.
 var. occidentalis, Watson.
maritimus, L.
Nevadensis, Watson.
pungens, Vahl.
riparius, Spreng.
rufus, Schrad.
subterminalis, Torr.
sylvaticus, L., var. digynus,
 Bœckl.

SCLERIA

triglomerata, Michx.
verticillata, Muhl.

GRAMINEÆ.

AGROPYRUM

caninum, R. & S.
dasystachyum, Vasey.
divergens, Nees.
 var. tenue, Vasey.
glaucum, R. & S., var. occidentale,
 V. & S.
repens, L.
tenerum, Vasey.
violaceum, Lange.

AGROSTIS

canina, L.
 var. paleata, Vasey, N. var.
exarata, Trin.
geminata, Trin.

microphylla, Steud.
oreophila, Trin.
perennans, Tuck.
scabra, Willd.
varians, Trin.
verticillata, Vill.
vulgaris, With.
   var. alba, Vasey.

AIRA

caryophyllea, L.
prœcox, L.

ALOPECURUS

alpinus, L.
geniculatus, L.
   var. aristulatus, Munro.
   var. robustus, Vasey.
Macounii, Vasey.
occidentalis, Scrib.
pratensis. L.

AMMOPHILA

arundinacea, Host.
longifolia, Vasey.

ANDROPOGON

provincialis, Lam.
scoparius, Michx.

ANTHOXANTHUM

odoratum, L.

ARCTAGROSTIS

latifolia, Griseb.
   var. Alaskensis, Vasey.

ARCTOPHILA

fulva, Rupt.
Læstadii, Rupt.
mucronata, Hack.

ARRHENATHERUM

avenaceum, P. B.

ARISTIDA

basiramea, Engelm.
dichotoma, L.
purpurea, Nutt.

ASPRELLA

hystrix, Willd.

AVENA

fatua, L.
pratensis, var. Americana, Scrib.
striata, Michx.

BECKMANNIA

erucæformis, Host., var. uniflorus,
   Scrib.

BOUTELOUA

hirsuta, Lag.
oligostachya, Torr.
racemosa, Lag.

BRACHYELYTRUM

aristatum, P. B.

BRIZA

media, L.

BROMUS

Aleutensis, Trin.
breviaristatus, Thurb.
ciliatus, L.
   var. ligulatus, Vasey.
   var. pauciflorus, Scrib.
Hookerianus, Thurb.
   var. minor, Scrib.
Kalmii, Gray.
Macounii, Vasey.
maximus, Desf.
mollis, L.
Orcuttianus, Vasey.
Pumpellianus, Scrib.
racemosus, L.
secalinus, L.

segetum, *Schlecht.*
Sitchensis, Bong.
subulatus, Led.
tectorum, L.

CATABROSA
aquatica, P. B.

CENCHRUS
tribuloides, L.

CHRYSOPOGON
nutans, Benth.

CINNA
arundinacea, L.
pendula, Trin.
    var. acutiflora, Vasey., N. sp.
    var. mutica, Vasey.

CYNODON
dactylon, Pers.

CYNOSURUS
cristatus, Linn.

DACTYLIS
glomerata, L.

DANTHONIA
Californica, Boland.
intermedia, Vasey.
spicata, Beauv.
unispicata, Munro.

DESCHAMPSIA
alba, Rœm. & Schultz.
atropurpurea, Scheele.
    var. latifolia, Scrib.
    var. minor, Vasey., N. var.
brevifolia, R. Br.
cæspitosa, P. B.
    var. arctica, Vasey.

    var. Bottanica, Vasey.
    var. longiflora, Trin.
    var. maritima, Vasey., N. var.
calycina, Presl.
elongata, Munro.

DEYEUXIA
æquivalis, Benth. & Hook.
Aleutica, Vasey.
borealis, Macoun., N. sp.
breviaristata, Vasey., N. sp.
Canadensis, Hook.
Columbiana, Macoun., N. sp.
confinis, Kunth.
crassiglumis, Vasey.
deschamsioides, Vasey.
Langsdorffii, Kunth.
Lapponica, Kunth.
Macouniana, Vasey., N. sp.
neglecta, Kunth.
    var. Americana, Vasey., N. var.
    var. brevifolia, Vasey., N. var
    var. robusta, Vasey, N. var.
Pickeringii, Vasey.
Porteri, Vasey.
purpurascens, Kunth.
rubescens, Vasey.
strigosa, Kunth.
Suksdorfii, Scrib.
sylvatica, Kunth.

DISTICHLIS
maritima, Raf.
    var. stricta, Thurb.

DUPONTIA
Fischeri, R. Br.
psilosantha, Rupt.

EATONIA
obtusata, Gray.
Pennsylvanica, Gray.

ELYMUS

Americanus, V. & S.
· arenarius, L.
Canadensis, L.
    var. glaucifolius, Gray.
Columbiana, Macoun.
condensatus, Presl.
dasystachys, Trin.
Macounii, Vasey.
mollis, Trin.
striatus, Willd.
Vancouverensis, Vasey.
Virginicus, L.
    var. submuticus, Hook.

ERAGROSTIS

major, Host.
minor, Host.
Purshii, Schrad.
reptans, Nees.

FESTUCA

duriuscula, Lam.
elatior, L.
microstachya, Nutt.
    var. divergens, Thurb.
    var. pauciflora, Scrib.
Myurus, L.
nutans, Willd.
occidentalis, Hook.
ovina, L.
    var. brevifolia, Watson.
    var. polyphylla, Vasey.
    var. vivipara, Gray.
Richardsonii, Hook.
rubra, L.
    var. villosa, Vasey.
scabrella, Torr.
subulata, Bong.
tenella, Willd.

FLUMINIA

arundinacea, Fries.

GLYCERIA

angustata, Ledeb.
arctica, Hook.
arundinacea, Kunth.
Canadensis, Trin.
distans, Wahl.
    var. airoides, Vasey.
elongata, Trin.
festucæformis, Reich.
fluitans, R. Br.
Lemmoni, Vasey.
maritima, Wahl.
nervata, Trin.
obtusa, Trin.
pallida, Trin.
pauciflora, Presl.
pumila, Vasey.

GRAPHEPHORUM

melicoides, Gray.
Wolfii, Vasey.

HIEROCHLOA

alpina, R. & S.
borealis, R. & S.
pauciflora, R. Br.

HOLCUS

lanatus, L.

HORDEUM

jubatum, L.
maritimum, With.
murinum, L.
pratense, Huds.
pusillum, Nutt.

KŒLERIA

cristata, Pers.
    var. gracilis, Gray.
    var. major, Vasey., N. var.

LEERSIA

oryzoides, Swartz.
Virginica, Willd.

LOLIUM

perenne, L.
temulentum, L.

MELICA

acuminata, Boland.
aristata, Thurb.
bulbosa, Geyer.
Harfordii, Boland.

MILIUM

effusum, L.

MUHLENBERGIA

diffusa, Schreb.
glomerata, Trin.
Mexicana, Trin.
sylvatica, T. & G.
Willdenovii, Trin.

MUNROA

squarrosa, Torr.

ORYZOPSIS

asperifolia, Michx.
Canadensis, Torr.
cuspidata, Scrib.
melanocarpa, Muhl.

PANICUM

agrostoides, Muhl.
capillare, L.
crus-galli, L.
  var. hispidum, Gray.
depauperatum, Muhl.
dichotomum, L.
  var. nitidum, Lam.
  var. pubescens, Gray.
glabrum, Gaud.
latifolium, L.
laxiflorum, Lam.
microcarpon, Muhl., var. sphæro-
  carpon, Vasey.
pauciflorum, Ell.

sanguinale, L.
scoparium, Lam.
virgatum, L.
xanthophysum, Gray.

PHALARIS

arundinacea, L.
Canariensis, L.

PHIPPSIA

algida, R. Br.
  var. monandra, Kunth.

PHLEUM

alpinum, L.
pratense, L.

PHRAGMITES

communis, Trin.

PLEUROPOGON

Sabinii, R. Br.

POA

abbreviata, R. Br.
alpina, L.
andina, Nutt.
  var. purpurea, Vasey., N. var
annua, L.
Bolanderi, Vasey.
cæsia, Smith.
  var. strictior, Gray.
Californica, Vasey.
cenisia, All.
compressa, L.
cuspidata, V. & S.
debilis, Torr.
  var. acutiflora, Vasey.
Eatoni, Watson.
flavicans, Ledeb.
glumaris, Trin.
Howellii, V. & S.
laxa, Hænke.
leptocoma, Trin.

Macounii, Vasey.
nemoralis, L.
Nevadensis, Vasey.
Nutkaensis, Presl.
pratensis, L.
purpurascens, Vasey.
serotina, Ehrh,
stenantha, Trin.
sub-aristata, Scrib.
tenuiflora, Nutt.
  var. Oregona, Vasey.
trivialis, L.

POLYPOGON

littoralis, Smith.
Monspeliensis, Desf.

SCHEDONNARDUS

Texanus, Steud.

SETARIA

glauca, Beauv.
Italica, Kunth.
verticillata, Beauv.
viridis, Beauv.

SPARTINA

cynosuroides, Willd.
gracilis, Trin.
juncea, Willd.
polystachya, Willd.
stricta, Roth., var. alterniflora,
  Gray.
  var. glabra, Gray.

SPOROBOLUS

asperifolius, Thurb.
cryptandrus, Gray.
cuspidatus, Scrib.
depauperatus, Scrib.
heterolepis, Gray.
vaginæflorus, Vasey.

STIPA

avenacea, Linn.
Columbiana, N. sp.
comata, Trin.
Richardsonii, Link.
  var. major, N. var.
spartea, Trin.
viridula, Trin.

TRIPLASIS

purpurea, Chapm.

TRISETUM

canescens, Buckl.
cernuum, Trin.
subspicatum, P. B.
  var. molle, Gray.

ZIZANIA

aquatica, L.

EQUISETACEÆ.

EQUISETUM

arvense, L.
hiemale, L.
lævigatum, A. Br.
limosum, L.
littorale, Kuhl.
maximum, Lam.
palustre L.
pratense, Ehrh.
robustum, A. Br.
scirpoides, Michx.
sylvaticum, L.
Telmateia, Ehrh.
variegatum, Schleich.

OPHIOGLOSSACEÆ.

BOTRYCHIUM

lanceolatum, Angs.
Lunaria, Swartz.

matricariæfolium, A. Br.
simplex, Hitch.
ternatum, Swartz.
  var. dissectum, Milde.
  var. lunarioides, Milde.
  var. obliquum, Milde.
Virginianum, Swartz.

OPHIOGLOSSUM

vulgatum, L.

FILICES.

ADIANTUM

pedatum, L.
  var. rangiferinum, Burgess.

ASPIDIUM

acrostichoides, Swartz.
aculeatum, Swartz.
  var. Braunii, Doell.
  var. scopulinum, Eaton.
Boottii, Tuckerm.
cristatum, Swartz.
  var. Clintonianum, Eaton.
Filix-mas, Swartz.
fragrans, Swartz.
Goldianum, Hook.
Lonchites, Swartz.
marginale, Swartz.
munitum, Kaulf.
Noveboracense, Swartz.
Oreopteris, Swartz.
rigidum, Swartz.
spinulosum, Swartz
  var. dilatatum, Hornem.
  var. intermedium, Eaton.
Thelypteris, Swartz.

ASPLENIUM

angustifolium, Michx.
ebeneum, Ait.
Filix-fœmina, Bernh.
  var. angustum, Eaton.

thelypteroides, Michx.
Trichomanes, L.
viride, Huds.

CAMPTOSORUS

rhizophyllus, Link.

CHEILANTHES

gracillima, Eaton.
lanuginosa, Nutt.

CRYPTOGRAMME

acrostichoides, R. Br.

CYSTOPTERIS

bulbifera, Bernh.
fragilis, Bernh.
montana, Bernh.

DICKSONIA

pilosiuscula, Willd.

GYMNOGRAMME

triangularis, Kaulf.

LOMARIA

spicant, Desv.
  var. serratum, Woll.

ONOCLEA

sensibilis, L.
  var. obtusilobata, Torr.
Struthiopteris, Hoffm.

OSMUNDA

cinnamomea, L.
Claytoniana, L.
regalis, L.

PELLÆA

atropurpurea, Link.
densa, Hook.
gracilis, Hook.

PHEGOPTERIS

alpestris, Mett.
calcarca, Fee.
Dryopteris, Fee.
hexagonoptera, Fee.
polypodioides, Fee.

POLYPODIUM

falcatum, Kellogg.
Scouleri, H. & G.
vulgare, L.

PTERIS

aquilina, L.
   var. lanuginosa, Bong.

SCHIZÆA

pusilla, Pursh.

SCOLOPENDRIUM

vulgare, Smith.
   var. marginatum, Moore.
   var. ramosum, Gray.

WOODSIA

glabella, R. Br.
hyperborea, R. Br.
Ilvensis, R. Br.
obtusa, Torr.
Oregana, Eaton.
scopulina, Eaton.

WOODWARDIA

Virginica, Smith.

MARSILIACEÆ.

MARSILIA

vestita, H. & G.

SALVINIACEÆ.

AZOLLA

Caroliniana, Willd.

LYCOPODIACEÆ.

LYCOPODIUM

alpinum, L.
annotinum, L.
   var. pungens, Desv.
clavatum, L.
complanatum, L.
dendroideum, Michx.
inundatum, L.
   var. Bigelovii, Tuck.
lucidulum, Michx.
sabinæfolium, Willd.
Selago, L.

SELAGINELLACEÆ.

SELAGINELLA

apus, Spring.
rupestris, Spring.
selaginoides, Link.

ISOETACEÆ.

ISOETES

echinospora, Durieu, var.
   Braunii, Engelm.
lacustris, L.
maritima, Underwood.
Nuttallii, A. Br.
riparia, Engelm.

www.ingramcontent.com/pod-product-compliance
Lightning Source LLC
Chambersburg PA
CBHW021627270326
41931CB00008B/909